W9-BTN-811

July 21, 1978
Notre Dame

To father
Michael Komachek
who knows
how to
steal from God,

Edward Fischer

Everybody Steals from God

Everybody Steals from God
communication as worship

Edward Fischer

UNIVERSITY OF NOTRE DAME PRESS

NOTRE DAME ~ LONDON

Copyright © 1977 by
University of Notre Dame Press
Notre Dame, Indiana 46656

Library of Congress Cataloging in Publication Data

Fischer, Edward.
   Everybody steals from God.

   Bibliography: p.
   1. Communication.   2.   Communication (Theology)
3.   Liturgics.   I.   Title.
P94.F5   001.5   77-3711
ISBN 0-268-00904-X

Manufactured in the United States of America

For Mary

hers is a free spirit

Contents

Why This Happened   ix

1: God Put Things in Good Shape   1

2: If It's in Good Shape, Here Is Why   11

3: From Ecclesiastical Prose, Deliver Us, O Lord   22

4: The Gospel according to Today as Found in the
   Mass Media   36

5: Films Can Offer More than Meets the Eye   52

6: A Journal Can Be More than "Dear Diary"   76

7: All Ritual Inherits the Aches of Communication   88

8: Education Can Prepare the Spirit for Worship   115

9: Living Is an Art–It Is Not Bookkeeping   142

   Reading That's Worth the Effort   165

   Films for the Spirit   168

Why This Happened

They came to the lectures and later encouraged me to put these thoughts into a book. As groups they were so varied that a list of them sounds suspicious, as though rigged: librarians, teachers, religious, journalists, film-makers, scientists, broadcasters, artists. Although varied in vocation they shared a common interest, an interest in lifting life, and it is that interest I speak of in these pages.

Since mass communication has been my line of trade for years, I needed scant urging to write about it. Worship was another matter. Never would I have had the courage to write of it except that liturgical scholars showed respect for my ideas of how communication and worship blend.

It started when Father Aiden Kavanaugh, O.S.B., currently of the faculty of the Yale Divinity School, asked that I speak at an international symposium called "Roots of Ritual." He felt that since ritual is a form of communication, the principles of communication practiced by professionals would be of interest to the ritualist. The scholars at the symposium were interested enough to ask that I repeat the lecture in various parts of the country. The manuscript of the lecture was printed in *Worship,* published at St. John's Abbey, Collegeville, Minnesota, in *Rond de Tafel,* Heeswijk-Dinter, Holland, and in *Questions Liturgiques,* Louvain, Belgium, as well as in the book made from the symposium: *The Roots of Ritual.* The managing editor of *Worship,* the Rev. Michael Marx, O.S.B., suggested that I do a series of articles about communication as worship. Then the Rev. James Shaughnessy gave added encouragement in seeking my advice on films being made by the Murphy Center for Liturgical Research at the University of Notre Dame.

What interested those men was the idea of design as worship. Design, as I use the word, is the most usual thing in creation and the basis of all communication, whether visual or verbal. Design is the template that I hold up to experience. We look at the world through templates of our own making and try to fit them over the realities of life. No fit is perfect, but even a sorry fit is better than none.

My hope is to present an ancient template in a new way, using current examples and a modern idiom. In holding up this particular template I am in fancy company, an experience that brings consolation and uneasiness all at once: Aristotle, Aquinas, and Kant saw design as an expression of God's will. Plato, who saw oneness in the multiverse of the world of things, said that "God ever geometrizes." The German physicist, Carl Gustav Jacob Jacobi, thought that "God ever arithmetizes." The British physicist, Sir James Jeans, observed that "The Great Architect of the Universe now begins to appear as a pure mathematician."

They sensed that creation is more than a mixture of atoms, that some design goes beyond proof, and that God is a rumor in the blood. In expressing wonder at the design of it all, they worshiped. They sang a *Te Deum* as surely as did Gerard Manley Hopkins when he wrote, "The world is charged with the grandeur of God."

Perhaps you will sense that I do not speak of God with ease. It's the embarrassment of the finite mind tampering with the infinite. I don't say much *about* God—that is the theologian's territory—but merely try to find Him in the context of my awareness. Above all I don't want to appear too conversant with the arrangements of the Almighty.

Everybody Steals from God

1: God Put Things in Good Shape

I saw it hanging there in the window of a secondhand book-shop in San Francisco and it has haunted me ever since. The long, narrow panel, covered with abstract designs similar in shape but varied in size, had an organic feeling about it. The motif was similar to that of muscle structure, a fitting analogy, because here was a rendering of the muscle of power. It was a chart showing the rise and fall of empires and civilizations over the past four thousand years.

I stood there looking at the history of billions of people whose lives must have seemed hectic to them and who proba-bly wondered if there is a plan to events. Or is life just chaos churned up? So much of history had to be recorded before this design, with its repeating motif, could be sketched to illustrate something Thucydides observed: "The kind of events that once took place will by reason of human nature take place again." Or as James Joyce said in our time, "History repeat-ing itself with a difference."

The histomap, as Rand McNally calls it, so struck me that I felt I had to have it, but the old man who owned the bookshop said it wasn't for sale; it was the last he had. He noticed my eagerness and commented on it. I told him I had come to the coast to lecture on the characteristics of good design at a con-ference of professional photographers and would like to use the histomap as an illustration. I explained that I teach design and see in this illustration one more piece of evidence that man-made design is only good when it bears the same characteristics found in all God-made design. To be more definite I asked him to imagine the motif of the histomap printed on cloth. Wouldn't it make an attractive drapery? He agreed and wondered what there was about the design that made it so pleasing.

That started me talking about the characteristics of good design, as I will later in these pages, characteristics that please us because we are hungry for them. They are ground into every atom of our bodies, I said. At that, the old man raised a sharp finger and said that he did not want to be "philosophically picayune"—yes, that is how he put it—but he felt I was making the characteristics of design sound as though they were added as an afterthought. He believed that instead of "ground into" I might better say "built into" because the characteristics of good design imbue nature and are not added as a dressing.

He was right, of course, they are so much a part of us that when we find them in another object it is like finding something of ourselves. I ended our conversation in the bookshop by quoting John Steinbeck's observation that, "Everything in the world must have design or the human mind rejects it." The old man and I parted agreeing with Steinbeck that normal human sensibilities recoil from nondesign, from chaos.

Design is important to me because, more than anything else, it makes me aware of God as creator and sustainer. I traveled the route Bernard Berenson describes in *Sunset and Twilight:* "Art educates us to appreciate nature, teaches us to appreciate in nature what with such difficulty and long training we have learned to appreciate in art, to find in nature to the highest degree the qualities that we find in art."

These qualities found in nature and in art are the qualities of effective design. By design I mean the pattern, plan, or order that imbues all of what God has made and the best of what man has made.

First, consider what God made. Or as William James used to say, "Come, let us gossip about the universe." When those who specialize in gossip about the universe, the scientists, begin to poke their curiosity into unexplored depths they are confronted by chaos, or so it seems to them. The more they explore, though, the more they uncover design.

Ignorance sees chaos that is not there. For instance, to most people who have lived on earth the weather seemed without plan, but that was because they didn't know enough about it. Now that thousands of weather stations report, each from its own limited view, and the reports are filed into a computer, the machine makes a design of the weather at a given moment, a delicate, graceful rose. Not many years ago astronomers still thought the Milky Way was chaotic. Now that they know more about it they find a breathless order. The scientists who discovered DNA, the molecule that carries the key to heredity, groped during their experiments in what seemed disheveled depths. As they discovered things, little by little, they built a model to make visible their findings, a model that developed as a double helix so well designed it could be exhibited in the Museum of Modern Art without looking out of place.

The same is true of mathematics. The mathematician starts groping in what seems chaos and eventually arrives at elegant form. Those of us ignorant in mathematics can enjoy a mathematical concept only when made visual in three-dimensional form, but the mathematician can have an aesthetic experience as his mind's eye sees the concept unfold in brilliant pattern.

This brings to mind a passage from Anaïs Nin's diary. She said that while leafing through the *Encyclopaedia Britannica* she came upon photographs of clay models of mathematical abstractions used to illustrate advanced concepts in geometry. She was struck by how much they resemble the sculptures of

Noguchi and began to see how many new forms in art are born of a scientific era. Her first awareness of this had come in the Museum of Natural History when she entered a room which featured magnified models of blood cells. Before knowing what they were she felt they were "the most beautifully designed, the most aesthetic forms I had seen, and I wondered whether our art concepts were born from some mysterious source such as the designs of our blood cells."

In her growing awareness of the excellent design found deep in creation Anaïs Nin is also traveling the route described by Bernard Berenson. This route grows more exciting now that microphotography reveals an unending succession of startling designs deep in the depths of things. Each improvement of camera, lens, film, lights, and microscope repeat, again and again, what was first observed with the naked eye, that nature is rich in superb design.

A microphotograph of brain cells appears as a sensitive oriental painting, sad and brooding, with birds tilted on bare branches, silhouetted in a winter's sunset. A speck of muscle photographed through a microscope is an exercise in delicate Japanese brushwork. The transverse section of a piece of coral enlarged many times resembles an elegantly flowered pattern in an old-fashioned carpet. A thin section of the spine of a sea urchin looks all the world like a lace doily made by an old-fashioned lady.

The amount of magnification and the kind of light used change the motif found in a speck of matter. For example, a bit of progesterone scarcely visible to the naked eye when magnified twenty times has the spikey motif of stalagmites and stalactites found in caves, but when magnified one hundred and twenty times the motif is one of soft and fanlike billows, like the spray of multicolored waves. So no matter how enlarged or how reduced, the design is always perfect, bringing to mind Swedenborg's doctrine that "nature exists entire in leasts."

The telescope repeats what the microscope says: there is no inept design in nature. Space exploration also confirms this. We knew all along that the earth as a whole must be a beautiful design, but not until recent years did we see a photograph of it showing cloud formations, water and land masses all working together in swirling, dramatic unified designs that have the look of masterful brushwork. Photographs of the earth taken from a satellite 569 miles in space resemble paintings by abstract expressionists. An ultraviolet photograph made through a lithium fluoride lens reveals that the earth's corona, a halo of oxygen flaring thousands of miles into space, is much like one of the later paintings of Kandinsky.

All modern painters are there to be found with a telescope and a microscope and a little patience. Metal alloy under a microscope is a Miro. Insulin crystals, magnified seventy times and reflecting a polarized light, look like a surrealistic golf course by Salvadore Dali. Hansen's bacillus, the cause of leprosy, is made up of bright swirling colors that look as though they have been lifted from a Van Gogh landscape. Microscopic views of lunar basalt might be by any one of several abstract expressionists. A photo of a piece of black opal taken through a microscope resembles the painting *Blue on a Point* by Sam Francis, a disciple of Jackson Pollock.

They are there, all right, either deep in or far out—Pollock, Klee, Mondrian. Yes, even Mondrian with his rectangles connected by straight lines, designs that seem too severely geometric for nature. Mondrian was not interested in reflecting nature; he was dedicated to dividing a picture plane into well-proportioned parts. He so sensitized designers with his work that he influenced architecture, packaging, magazine layout, and just about all areas of design. Mondrian would have been surprised to know that when he walked along a sidewalk he stepped on billions of his kind of design: photograph a chemical curing compound through a microscope with a certain kind of light, and, lo, there is a Mondrian! Iron crystal slightly oxidized and magnified ten thousand times is a sensitive arrangement of rectangles with all of the just proportion of a Mondrian. There are fish in the Shedd Aquarium in Chicago with Mondrians on their sides, or so I have been told.

Bernard Berenson believed that art exists to help us see nature better. That is a religious approach, because it places God's work above man's. It is unfortunate, though, that he never found anything of nature in nonrepresentational paintings and so he never really accepted them. Had he kept in touch with the development of microphotography and macrophotography he would have noticed that in the depths and in the far reaches of nature all forms appear nonrepresentational to the untrained eye, and yet they really represent something, they really are a part of nature.

A painter who has gone stale and catches himself repeating himself could do worse than spend a few hours looking at specimens through a microscope. They can be from any area of science—botany, zoology, geology—it makes no difference, they will be rich in design. Ideas are everywhere. Everybody steals from God.

Design in nature isn't static, an impression I may have given by using examples from still photography. Motion picture cameras reveal design in movement. Through time-lapse photography flowers have been shown to do a dance as they grow and with music added to the sound track the effect on the screen is charming. A documentary about microphotography, *The World You Never See,* used time-lapse photography— exposing one frame every fifteen minutes instead of the normal twenty-four frames a second—to show that as mushrooms grow they move with the grace of a cluster of tutus in a ballet. As much as sixty years ago a scientist attached a harness to a goldfish and to a device that wrote on a revolving drum, revealing that the fish choreographed a marked daily rhythm.

Scientists don't agree on how much design there is in the universe. Among physicists there are those who believe in cause and effect and those, a majority, aware of randomness in the movements of the atom, who wonder if chanciness is not also true of the universe at large. Einstein held to cause and effect, saying he did not believe God plays dice with the universe. He believed that randomness seems present because physicists have not yet explored their subject sufficiently.

No matter which side is correct there is still a great deal of predictable order as reflected in these events:

When the Russians landed a rocket on the moon, September 13, 1959, the newspapers made quite a point of saying they had calculated the landing to within eighty-four seconds. The spaceship, Pioneer 10, traveled twenty-one months at 82,000 miles an hour for 513 million miles to reach Jupiter sixty seconds ahead of schedule. A little later when Skylab III traveled 35 million miles during its eighty-four days in space the announcement was made, and made well in advance, that the astronauts would splash down at 10:17 a.m. EST. Not 10:15 or 10:20, mind you, but 10:17. And so they did. By then this was so accepted, so taken for granted that order and pattern and plan and cause and effect would carry the day, that the television networks did not bother to give live coverage to the splashdown.

Some randomness in order may make a difference in the precision of science, but not in aesthetics. Science is so precise that on January 1, 1977 the official clocks around the world were slowed down by one second to adjust to the fact that the aging earth slowed down one second in the preceding twelve months. In aesthetics a touch of the random here and there adds to the pleasure. Handmade objects tend to be more pleasing than machine-made because they are less severely precise. Even in computer art the finished drawing is more interesting if some randomness is programmed into the project. The surprises in an atom's habits may be analogous to jazz's syncopation, getting an accent where you don't expect it or getting a strong beat where a weak beat might be. Part of the delight of a

Sousa march is the unexpected accent notes. Fürtwangler favored a flexible tempo. Watercolorists are always looking for the "happy accident." All of this means that in art, and maybe in nature, too, it is good to have a certain playfulness going on within the order, but the order must be there all the same.

For years a scientific interest in the design of nature overshadowed an aesthetic interest. The word *aesthetic* seemed to be used only when applied to something man-made. Recently, though, there has been a revival of interest in the aesthetics of nature. For example, in 1971 a group of Harvard faculty and students began meeting to study relationships and similarities of forms in natural phenomena. They called themselves the philomorphs, or form-lovers. An article about the philomorphs in the Fall 1974 issue of *Harvard Today* said:

> Few have asked why lightening, trees, arteries and rivers each branch in similar patterns and what cause there might be for their underlying harmony. Why does wood in a tree trunk have the appearance of water flowing? Why do cracks in mud and markings on a giraffe arrange themselves like films in a froth of bubbles? Why do the fiddle-heads of ferns, stellar galaxies and water emptying from a bathtub spiral in such similar ways? Why do so many natural processes, at first glance so different, appear to act as metaphors for each other, echoing a few formal themes over and over?

In their concerns for the designs of creation the Harvard professors are moving into the realms of mental health and religious sensitivity, whether they know it or not. For instance, an awareness of the design of things in the universe can make the universe more acceptable. Monks in Macedonia who ran a lunatic asylum observed through the years that one kind of lunatic is easier to cure than another. They said, long before Western psychiatrists discovered it, that there is greater hope for the neurotic, the man who is at war with himself but accepts the universe, than for the psychotic, who accepts himself but rejects the universe.

The study of design of the things of the universe can lead to gratitude for the privilege of having been born into it. The discovery of design can lead to a sense of security in the scheme of God's providence. As soon as you get a hunch that there is a will of God loose in the universe, you relax, knowing you are not careening down the mountain road all out of control.

All of this is good for mental health and for life of the spirit—which isn't something *other* than daily living, but it *is* daily living with an added dimension. It is living with both feet on the ground and both eyes open and being aware that while there is more than meets the eye, whatever that "moreness" is can be discerned in what does meet the eye.

To see God in the design of things leads to the quiet prayer of wonder. It brings a comfort that Augustine called the *tranquillitas ordinis,* the tranquility of order.

Artists, too, help in this religious formation, whether they realize it or not. Through the centuries Chinese artists have said that they do not imitate nature, but work like nature. Picasso said the same thing. They mean they do not imitate nature in a photographic way but put into their work the characteristics of design found in nature. That's the subject of the next chapter.

We might well close this one by quoting two scientists who, in turn, quote Gyorgy Kepes, a designer. Henry Margenau and David Bergamini, in their book *The Scientist,* wrote:

> The work of the scientist is based upon a conviction that nature is basically orderly. Evidence to support this faith can be seen with the naked eye—in the design of a honeycomb or a mollusk's shell—but scientists come upon order at every level of being. The physicist finds it in the arrangement of atoms on a needle's point, the entomologist in the structure of a mosquito's eye, the crystallographer in the architecture of crystals. The scientist's primary interest in order is in the information it supplies: the orderly laws of what, why, and when. And when he finds the order he seeks he

often finds beauty as well. The landscape, microscopic or macroscopic, that engrosses the scientist has symmetry, grace, and balance. It is a landscape, according to MIT professor Gyorgy Kepes, that can delight "the scientist's brain, the poet's heart, the painter's eye . . . that has both the character of information and the quality of poetic vision."

2: If It's in Good Shape, Here Is Why

While doing a film for NASA I needed help from scientists. One day while checking the script with one of them, I pointed to a shelf of his textbooks and remarked that with any one I could teach a course in design. This so aroused the scientist's curiosity that I had to explain, then and there, what a designer could learn about art from a science book. He found the idea especially interesting because his daughter was studying art in Italy and until then he had seen no relationship between his work and hers, and she hadn't either. Both probably had heard so often about the cultural gap between art and science that they were resigned to it. Anyway, it was evident that we would not continue with the film script until I had described the characteristics of design reflected in illustrations in science texts.

So I explained to the scientist the same things that the old man and I had spoken of in the bookshop in San Francisco. The trouble with such explanations is the trouble with teaching any subject: you are forced to do something artificial; for the sake of making clear, you must fragment the subject, label the parts, define the labels, and hope that when all is said and done everybody will put everything back together and see it in a new light.

With hesitancy I fragmented design into four characteristics:

11

unity, variety, balance, harmony. These characteristics are desirable wherever design is found, and it is found wherever you look. The mass media use design in newspaper and magazine makeup, advertising layout, photography, and in the composition of pictures on television and motion picture screens. Commerce uses it in all products ranging from sports cars to saltcellars. Around the home design is reflected in interior decoration and in landscaped gardens. Religion uses it in buildings, symbols, and ritual. Design is at the heart of architecture, oil painting, the dance, all art forms.

Fortunately, the same characteristics apply to all design, no matter where found. So the characteristics of good design, once learned, open the eyes to many aspects of life. It is like learning any language; after the vocabulary and grammar are acquired they can be used to read a variety of things.

When a language is learned, verbal or nonverbal, the problem also is to develop a discrimination that senses when the language is well-used or abused. This is harder than learning the language, because discrimination seeps in subtly. It comes largely through osmosis, being "caught" from teachers, friends, the media, cultures, travel, the whole environment. More of this later, but first I'll explain what I mean by unity, variety, balance, and harmony.

Unity is the most important characteristic of a design. The unifying idea is the life-giving force that holds a design together. Without it there is nondesign, chaos. Stacks of bricks, stone, and lumber scattered about a building site are chaotic and become a design only when unity is imposed as they are assembled according to an architect's idea. The power of his idea, the force of the design, could vary from the meanness of a hovel to the grandeur of a palace.

Unity comes from having something dominate. Whatever dominates is called a motif or theme. It is all right to have several motifs or themes in one work, just so that one is major and the rest are minor. For example, in architecture the Gothic arch, Romanesque pillar, and Doric column are effective motifs, but if all were used with equal force in the same building, the effect would not be a super-design but super-chaos.

Artists need a strong sense of unity. Their ability to confer unity is not just a physical skill but something of a moral force, too. That is because anything that helps us sense the oneness of things has a moral dimension that makes it worth having around no matter what its flaws.

Surely there must be a moral basis to an aesthetic experience, that excitement of the spirit that comes from being in the presence of something unified with exceptional grace. The spirit can be excited and uplifted by a work of art even when the subject matter is not uplifting: The hoodlums in *On the Waterfront,* the fight crowd in *The Set Up,* and the revelers in *La Dolce Vita* are not uplifting people but the films about them are. In a work of art the artist is more on trial than his subject matter when he strives to stamp his work with a sense of "rightness," of which unity is one characteristic.

A hunger for unity may be the ultimate hunger because unity is so much of the created plan. The physical scientist, whose subject is God's creation, finds, as we have seen, a unifying plan in everything from an atom to a galaxy. The social scientist, however, whose subject is people, finds much disunity, because people use their free will to spurn unity in a way the rest of creation can't.

Yet the hunger for unity persists. That is why when a unified work brings an aesthetic experience it lessens the hunger a bit; it gives consolation because the artist's display of order raises our hopes in ourselves, in our possibilities. A work of art makes us realize that things need not fly off in all directions at once, because here is definite proof that things can live in happy conjunction, imitating the unity that imbues creation.

If this hunger for unity is not at least partly satisfied we are in trouble. Robert Frost saw it as a mental health problem and said in a filmed lecture in his own craggy, exaggerated way: "You know, I've often said that every poem solves something for me in life. I go so far as to say that every poem is a momentary stay against the confusion of the world.

"Any psychiatrist will tell you that making a basket, or making a horseshoe, or giving anything form gives you a confidence in the universe . . . that it has form, see?

"When you talk about your troubles and go to somebody about them, you're just a fool. The best way to settle them is to make something that has form, because all you want to do is get a sense of form."

Variety without unity is chaotic, just as unity without variety is dull. To bring an interesting order out of chaos an artist develops his theme or motif in varied ways.

Variety is important in design, and in life, because we have a hunger for it. The hunger is there because variety is a characteristic of design found in all creation. For example, every snowflake has the same motif but no two in all the blizzards of all time have been identical. Snowflakes photographed under a microscope vary in appearance from that of an iron Teutonic military decoration to an elegant, gold piece of jewelry. An enlarged fragment of one of those flakes may resemble a delicate, colorful mosaic that makes the mosaics of Ravenna crude in comparison. A fingerprint is another example of endless variety. To the untrained eye every fingerprint has the same unifying motif of rhythmic concentric swirls, but the trained eye sees that no two fingerprints are identical.

Rhythm is sometimes listed as one of the basic characteristics of good design. I put it here as an aspect of variety, for rhythm by its nature is varied. It is an integral part of nature from ripples in water to mountain ranges and from phases of the moon to the seasons of the year. These are evident rhythms, but there are so many hidden ones that Ritchie Ward wrote a book on the subject, *The Living Clocks*. In the opening pages he says that the rhythms in some living things occur every thousandth of a second, in others every second or every hour. Most rhythms are approximately twenty-four hours. Some are weekly and some monthly. In rare organisms the event may repeat every seven years, or even every seventeen. No matter how seldom or how often the repetition, a recurring rhythm is basic to creation.

Balance in art, as in life, is a stay against vertigo; a lack of it causes uneasiness. We crave balance because it, too, is an essential part of nature. Ecologists are filled with stories of disturbing chain reactions that come when nature is thrown out of balance: a shortage of birds in an area may allow the number of insects to increase to a point where certain plants are destroyed and this destruction causes another imbalance, bringing to mind the couplet: Great fleas have little fleas upon their backs to bite them. And little fleas have lesser fleas and so on *ad infinitum*.

In a design, balance may be formal or informal, just so long as it is there. Formal balance is symmetrical: whatever is on one side of the center is a mirror image of what is on the other side. Informal balance is asymmetrical, yet it has the *feeling* of balance. It can be created in several ways: A large object near the center can be balanced by a smaller object at a greater distance from the center. (On a seesaw, the larger boy moves in toward the center and the smaller boy moves out toward the end of the board and so they balance.) A small area of strong color balances a large area of faint color. A small animate object balances a large inanimate object. A smaller object of unusual shape balances a large object of usual shape.

Informal balance is preferred to formal balance these days, but that was not always the case. It used to be that formal balance was the style in architecture, interior decorating, landscape gardening, newspaper makeup, advertising layout, ballet, and other man-created things that now tend toward informal designs.

Harmony has to do with fitness and rightness. An artist is a person who makes things "right," using right in the sense that he makes all things work together in harmony.

Harmony is the hallmark of the professional. By professional I don't mean someone who gets paid for his work, but someone who works from a certain spirit, a certain attitude of wanting things "right." Some people work all their lives at something for pay and still act as though it is their first day on the job. They are the eternal amateurs. A professional in spirit has a strong sense of harmony. He makes things add up; he has control, he makes things "work" whether they be short stories, restaurants, or colleges. He has a way of doing things, as the Greeks said, so that nothing can be rightly added and nothing rightly taken away. As an excellent example, an Olympic figure skater performs so that nothing can be rightly added and nothing rightly taken away.

Harmony shows up in a million ways: The kind of typeface used to advertise a tractor ought not be the same as the kind used to advertise a perfume; the kind of paper selected for wedding invitations ought not be the same as that used to advertise a fire sale; the music on the sound track ought to be right for what is happening on the screen; the size and shape of a painting ought to work well with the size and the shape of the wall it hangs on because if it doesn't that is unfair to the painting and to the wall. In lack of harmony there is always an element of unfairness.

The Greeks, so sensitive to harmony, discovered that mathematical relationships in music and in the visual arts influence the quality of those arts. They found that strings of certain lengths give off certain harmonious sounds and that certain proportions are more harmonious than others: the how-muchness of mathematics influencing the how-effectiveness of art, quantity influencing quality.

Alfred North Whitehead considered this discovery a landmark in the history of human thought because seeing a relationship between art and mathematics led the Greeks to a more general philosophic concept. Whitehead described the concept as "that of the general interconnectedness of things, which transforms the manifoldness of the many into the unity of the one."

The Greeks suspected that certain proportions in painting and sculpture and architecture and in the rhythms of music also recur in biological life. The Greeks were right in their intuitions: The theme of Matila Ghyka's book *The Geometry of Art and Life* is that modern biology proves the Greeks correct. Ghyka wrote, "The use of Geometry in the study and classification of crystals is obvious, but it is only lately that its role in the study of Life and Living Growth has begun to be recognized."

Books on mathematics sometimes deal with the proportions of the areas in Mondrian's paintings and with the proportions of the Parthenon's facade. Mathematicians are interested in the many subtle ways Mondrian works into his paintings proportions of approximately two to three, known to the Greeks as the golden section. The Parthenon also reflects the golden section as well as the five to seven to eleven ratio, a proportion that the Greeks found harmonious for a three-dimensional structure.

The Greeks' interest in harmony made them aware of the optical illusion called the visual center. The visual center is where the eye "feels" the center to be, a little above true center. So the Greeks made adjustments in their work to cater to this peculiarity in the eye's way of seeing. For example, if the long steps in front of the Parthenon were truly parallel to the ground they would seem to sag somewhat in the center; to avoid this the builders arched them ever so slightly at the center. If the base of the Parthenon's pediment were truly parallel with the ground it would seem to sag and so it, too, was arched ever so slightly.

The Greeks, so harmony conscious, made other adjustments to cater to the eye's way of seeing things. For example, the two outer pillars on the Parthenon are tilted inward slightly, tilted to the extent that if the axis of each were extended they would meet about a mile above the building. Had the two outside columns been truly parallel to each other they would have appeared stiff and strained, almost as though they were trying to bow outward.

The capitals of Greek columns are also a part of harmony, for they are transitions that soften the blow of the thrust of the column meeting the base of the pediment, just as the plinth softens the thrust of the column meeting the floor.

The Greeks noticed that in nature there is always a transitional effect: a tree does not penetrate the ground with the harshness that a post does, because there is a swelling at the base of the tree that softens the blow, just as there is a swelling at the base of limbs, branches, twigs, and leaves, all transitions that make for harmony.

Sometimes something is made inharmonious on purpose to jolt, to shock, to get attention. The advertisement showing a gigantic egg with a chain wrapped around it, sitting in the middle of a desert, made you stop and look and so served its purpose. You would not care to hang such a picture on a wall; you would soon tire of having it around. It is a gimmick. Perhaps a definition of a gimmick would be: anything that ignores one of the characteristics of good design—unity, variety, balance, harmony. Whatever ignores these carries an abrasiveness that attracts attention to itself. Abrasiveness has its place, now and then, but a little goes a long way.

So much of man's creative effort now goes into gimmicks. Some of the best imaginations of our time are used to dream up television commercials. The best of the commercials bring the minor delight that cleverness brings and they hold the attention in a way that new gimmicks hold it. Yet their aims are trivial: they exist to promote gasoline, hair spray, and beer.

Many current motion pictures have interests nearly as trivial as television commercials. One film critic, sated by the insubstantial, said that we need to keep praising the likes of Bergman, Fellini, Truffaut, and Antonioni because they still address themselves to the problems of the soul: God, loneliness, death, love. They settle down and try to explain man's estate to man. They put into their work the insight that F. Scott Fitzgerald said is found in literature: "You discover that your longings are universal longings, that you're not lonely and isolated from anyone. You belong. That is a part of the beauty of all literature."

Trivial art has no moral strength. I do not mean moral in the sense of preachment or of Victorian prudery; I mean it in the sense of aim or ideal. If something is exceptionally well done it has embedded in its very existence the aim of lifting the common denominator rather than catering to it. To get back to the Parthenon, it had the strength of an ideal. The medieval cathedral was another ideal. Around these buildings there must have been chaos galore, but there they stood as symbols to be looked up to, a definite proof that it can be done, that man can lift himself above chaos if only he will try. Trivial art lets itself off too easily; it doesn't carry its own weight.

Artists say that the thing that keeps a picture alive, keeps it interesting to have around, is not so much the subject matter as it is the basic abstract design. This idea can be a stumbling block to students because subject matter is more recognizable than basic abstract design.

To help them see past the subject matter I use two slides. One is of a photograph that appeared on the cover of the Louisville *Courier-Journal* Sunday magazine, showing a monk in the cloisters at Gethsemani, Kentucky. It is a strong picture because it is held together by a strong motif, the Gothic arch, repeated in varied ways. The arch is in the windows, and in the ceiling, and is hinted at in the shadows; it is repeated in the monk's raised cowl and appears upside down in his ample sleeves and echoes in the folds of his robes. Over and over the Gothic arch appears, in a variety of ways.

If that same monk, the subject matter, went outside and stood by a mulberry bush his picture might appear inside the magazine, but it would not be apt to appear on the cover because he would seem less interesting; he would not have the Gothic in the architecture accenting the Gothic in his own design. The basic abstract design would be less strong.

The other slide that helps make the point about the importance of design over subject matter shows the most popular photograph taken in World War II. Of the hundreds of thousands made, many of them of important actions, the one that gives promise of living longest, the Iwo Jima flag-raising, is not a picture of the most important action in the war.

The basic abstract design of the Iwo Jima photograph is a unifying triangular motif that is echoed in a variety of ways with good informal balance and all elements working in harmony. First of all, the flagstaff thrusts across the picture in a dramatic diagonal, dividing the picture into two large triangles, but not of equal size because to divide a picture plane into equal parts makes a division that lacks subtlety. The wind blew the flag into the picture, fortunately; if it had blown the other way the flag would have pointed out of the picture, leading the eye out, a flaw in design. By happy accident the wind spanked the flag in such a way as to fold it into two triangles, one large and one small. The Marines hoisting the flagstaff fall into a triangular grouping; the one who draws apart also forms a triangle, the space between his legs is triangular and he thrusts the base of the staff against a triangular rock formation.

A news photographer made several shots of the same subject, a group of Marines raising a flag at Iwo Jima. Almost any of the photographs might have appeared in the newspapers the next day and then been forgotten, except that one of them had such excellent basic abstract design that it lived to become the inspiration for a postage stamp, a motion picture, and a statue in the park.

When learning to apply the characteristics of good design, harmony is usually the last mastered and often never is. Unity, variety, and balance can be applied in cold blood from out of the head, but harmony comes from the depths of the sensibilities. Harmony presents a problem in teaching because it is difficult to explain and sometimes its presence or absence is impossible to prove. As someone said, you can't prove that one poem is better than another.

Since harmony is subtle and frustrating to consider, I will give it more attention in the next chapter, the one about the use of words. I find that in verbal communication more than in visual communication the deficiencies in a sense of harmony show through. It is in the sense of harmony that taste and discernment and professionalism are revealed.

3: From Ecclesiastical Prose, Deliver Us, O Lord

I was asked to give a talk to a university's arts and letters advisory council whose membership included a gallery curator, an actress, a film director, and so on. Since my talk was to be about the problems of teaching writing, I focused on the written word, although I also teach design. Later, a member of the advisory council, the chief designer for an auto firm, said, "I don't know anything about writing, but everything you said about it I am saying all day long to my young designers."

I know what he meant because I say much the same things in a writing course as in a design course. In all creative work, as in all of life, the problem is to bring an effective order out of chaos. The order comes from groping towards the characteristics of good design. Groping is the right word, for as the Greeks said, truth is hidden in the depths and is brought to the surface with a struggle.

Once a student learns design, I find it easier to teach him how to write. The important thing is that he develop his sense of good order, of significant form, to a high degree. Once that happens, he makes things add up because he feels uneasy with chaos flying in all directions. This attitude carries over from one art to another, God willing. At least it does with the best artists. When Hemingway was asked who taught him how to write, he named almost as many painters and musicians as writers. Flannery O'Connor said that she and other fiction writers often paint, not that they expect to be good at it, but they find that painting helps them *see*. At the end of a symphony rehearsal, John Pritchard felt pleased with his performance as conductor, but his mentor, Fritz Busch, said, "This is all very well, but when did you last go to a picture gallery."

In this chapter I am ignoring unity, variety, and balance, even though they apply to a piece of writing as much as to the visual arts. I want to focus on harmony, where the problem most often lies when using words. It is in the sense of harmony that taste is tested. A piece of writing might develop a unified theme unfolding in a varied and balanced way, and yet for lack of discernment the mood might be tasteless, or at least inert. Examples of such sludgy writing can easily be dredged up from federal prose. The word *gobbledygook,* now in the dictionary, was coined by a congressman vexed at the heavy, dull, unclear, and sometimes pretentious prose accumulated by bureaucracy. As a farm boy he had heard the noise made by frightened turkey gobblers and found that federal prose when read aloud had much the same sound.

Ecclesiastical prose gets more attention in these pages than federal prose because its sins against harmony are greater offenses. When a churchman tries to communicate something about the Almighty in a graceless way he lowers life, a lack of harmony if there ever was one.

This sounds as though I make a severe distinction between the sacred and the secular, but I don't. It's just that anyone who believes that God is the author of life just has to follow through and believe that whatever lifts life is good and whatever lowers it is evil. If lifting life is reverential it is a form of worship, and so the quality of the work separates the sacred from the profane even more than the subject matter of the work. A nun tells her art students that a well-painted apple does more for the honor and glory of God than a badly done madonna. This startles them because they are accustomed to thinking of the *what* more than of the *how* when dividing the sacred from the secular. And so I am sparing bureaucrats, lawyers, sociologists, and other perpetrators of gobbledygook and focusing attention on theologians, who should be more concerned than anyone with doing things well.

Theology books have a special tendency toward heavy-handedness, especially those influenced by sociology and psychology. It is possible to read page after page without sensing one wisp of the human soul behind the sludgy sentences. Theologians often handle matters of the spirit in a way George Orwell said bureaucrats would have written a line in Ecclesiastes had they had the chance: "The race is not to the swift, nor the battle to the strong . . ." would have come down to us by way of bureaucracy as, "Objective consideration of contemporary phenomena compels the conclusion that success or failure in competitive activities exhibits no tendency to be commensurate with innate capacity."

The beautiful lines of the psalm, "The Lord is my shepherd, I shall not want. He maketh me to lie down in green pastures;" have been badly damaged in a new translation which says, "In verdant pastures he gives me repose." Those words *verdant* and *repose* made the translator feel he had done a good day's work.

So much of the New Theology reads like an eye chart. A wag said that the Gospel according to the New Theology might sound this way: Jesus said unto them, "Who do you say that I am?" And they replied, "You are the eschatological manifestation of the ground of our being, the kerygma in which we find the ultimate meaning of our interpersonal relationships." And Jesus said, "What!"

A shelf of theology books may not hold one thrill of rapture. How ironic. They speak of the most thrilling subject matter in existence, and yet they are flabby and dull. Theologians might pay more attention to art in hopes some of its aliveness will rub off.

At one Catholic college a theologian committed so much gobbledygook and so damaged the language in his classroom that it became a grim joke around the campus. The student newspaper published a parody of his prose:

> A community, characterized by Christian love, presents a unique opportunity for growth and development. Challenging the whole person, total involvement demands a recognition of the common humanity shared by others. Initial commitment leads to in-depth dialogue, and the ensuing interpersonal relationships will lead to many a meaningful experience.
>
> The privilege of preparing one's role in society, the extension of community, demands responsibility on the part of the individual. Superficiality and mediocrity must be replaced with significant and relevant ideals. Outmoded structures must be replaced by creative attempts to reach the desired goal of total personalism. The conscience of mankind must react positively to this search for identity and encourage the process of becoming, lest man's true self be lost in meaningless tradition of existential apathy. (*Seton Journal,* Mount St. Joseph, Ohio)

An English monk, Dom Bede Griffiths, expressed his concern about the abuse of language in theology and philosophy. He said that while reading *Ethics* and *Politics* in the original Greek he was delighted to observe that since Aristotle had to form a philosophical language out of the material of ordinary human speech, there is in his writing the sense of contact with human life and human needs, something absent in much of modern thought. Here is a case of language growing organically out of the needs of human life, in contrast with manufactured language of a civilization losing its roots in common life.

Another English monk, Dom Hubert van Zeller, said that as a boy he was weighted down by the pious prose in the devotional books that his grandmother wrote. He found the experience useful, though, because when he came to write spiritual books of his own he decided to use the idiom of every day to urge the people of every day to embark upon a spirituality of every day.

This is a problem of the ages. In the fifteenth century an anonymous Englishman said in *The Cloud of Unknowing,* a quaint book about prayer, the fewer words the better, "Yea, and if it be but a little word of one syllable, methinks it better than two." He observed that we are most honest in our use of words when we are most deeply distressed. We yell, "help," and "fire," and "stop."

Monsignor Ronald Knox, who always showed a concern for language, proved in his own work that it is possible to write at some altitude without dehumanizing communication. Evelyn Waugh said that in all of Knox's prose his speaking voice is always audible.

His speaking voice is always audible—that is worth noting. The speaking voice is the natural way of communicating. Writing is an artificial method. Of all the people who have walked the earth only a small percentage learned to write. Of those who learned, many have made the skill more artificial than it need be, dehumanizing it until the sense of one human being trying to get through to another human being is lost in the clutter.

Charts have been designed, with tongue in cheek, to help federal bureaucrats and social scientists grind out triple talk with the least amount of thought and effort. I have devised such a system for anyone writing about ecclesiastical matters. Here are three paragraphs of twelve words each. Select one word at random from each paragraph. Repeat the process often enough and you may be the author of a book of theology.

1. traditional, meaningful, comparative, proximate, tentative, total, viable, relevant, valid, cognitive, societal, eschatological

2. existential, theological, liturgical, pastoral, empirical, dynamic, unchanging, charismatic, hueristic, motoric, environmental, kerygmatic

3. hierarchy, norms, commitment, challenge, dialogue, role, options, transition, involvement, alienation, orientation, revelation

Notice how you can accumulate impressive sentences: A viable unchanging hierarchy, a meaningful charismatic dialogue, and a relevant liturgical challenge are needed today by the people of God. Failing this we shall be cast into the cognitive environmental role that confronts us with a comparative theological option capable of solution only by total pastoral commitment.

Since completing that chart I have learned that the Rev. David E. Babin presented a similar list at a diocesan meeting of clergy. He included *authentic, incarnational, communal, ecumenical, implemental, Chardinian, encounter.*

Such gobbledygook gained respectability in the Church during the past twenty-five years, its rise coinciding with the growing of regard for the social sciences. Before that there was "sermonese" all right, but of a different sort. The old-fashioned pastor used glittering generalities, sentimentality, and hell and brimstone as his main thrusts. His rolling, sonorous sentences reflected his Latin schooling and the Irish influence on the American clergy.

If there is one thing worse than the old-fashioned sermonese and the pseudo-social science gobbledygook, it is the language of a churchman trying to be "with" it and not knowing how. In a parish bulletin an article was headed, "Humility Is Cool." Can such articles as "Hope Is Hip" and "Grace Is Groovy" be far behind? Such faddish language, as all fads, is a form of spiritual virus that sweeps across the country. Some people are more susceptible to it than others, just as some are more susceptible to Asian flu. Only those who have built up their resistance have a chance of avoiding infection from either.

A faddish virus can sweep the country in an instant with the help of television. When John Dean III said, "at that point in time," the phrase started popping up in many a television interview. The word *escalate* became popular after President Johnson used it in connection with the Vietnam War. During the fuel crisis William Simon spoke of "the energy crunch" and from "that point in time" the word *crunch* found its way into strange places. I don't know which politician first committed *Vietnamize*. The computer folk gave us *in-put* and *feedback*. Right now *hopefully* and *basically* are dropped into sentences with abandon. In student papers, *societal, relevant,* and *lifestyle* are doing well.

A survey of college couples who live together, unmarried, quoted some of them saying they have "a meaningful interpersonal relationship," an expression used freely by anyone who has had a class in psychology or has been exposed to someone who has. The *New Yorker* based a cartoon on this: a young couple in a small boat approach what used to be called The Tunnel of Love but now bears the sign, The Tunnel of Meaningful Interpersonal Relationships.

Fads do pass. Some clichés go away. In the nineteenth century when an Englishman used the word *sentimentality* he was apt to say, "Wordsworthian sentimentality," something no longer heard except in sophomore English Lit. A few years ago the fad was to tack *wise* onto any noun that got in the way—*businesswise, weatherwise, moneywise*—but that is not heard much anymore and when it is there is something almost quaint about it. It's consoling to remember that a fad, like a virus, will run its course.

The general dehumanization of language, the spirit with which language is used, is much more destructive than the annoying fad words that come and go. Some professionals are beginning to be concerned about this abuse. I first became aware of this concern after completing a film, *The War on Gobbledygook*. Its first booking came from the Defense Information School, where military men are taught how *not* to write military prose, and its second booking came from a law school. Later, I published an article using legal prose as an example of dehumanized writing and received letters from several lawyers encouraging me to say it again. As this chapter was being written a letter came from the dean of a law school asking that I talk to his students about treating the language with care.

Dr. Lois De Bakey, the sister of two surgeons, Michael and Ernest De Bakey, said in the *New England Journal of Medicine* that physicians use too much jargon. Among the changes she suggests is that instead of *agrypnia, cephalalgia, cholelithiasis, emesis,* and *prexia,* doctors should say *insomnia, headache, gallstones, vomiting,* and *fever.* She thinks that *"in extremis* is a pretentious expression for dying."

This matter of trying to cover up reality with jargon shows up in so many ways. Countries are no longer backward, but "developing" or "emerging." Nobody is poor, only "underprivileged." Those underprivileged folks don't live in slums anymore, but reside in the "inner city."

When it comes to cover-up jargon, teachers can hold their own with the best of them. Back on the farm in Kentucky I was dumb, but now I would be "an underachiever" in comparison with my "peer group." This is all part of a diplomatic language that teachers use when holding summit meetings with parents. Teachers say the child needs to be "enriched" for better "peer-group adjustment." He is "capable of doing better" and with help may soon be "working at his own level." The teacher never says the little monster is goofing off but, instead, says, "he could make better use of time." Teachers never come right out and say the kid has a mean streak, but they hint at it by commenting that he has "difficulty in getting along with others." He is not selfish, it is just that he "seldom shares with others." He is not rude, he is just "inconsiderate of others." If he is a young hoodlum, he "does not always respond to behavioral guidance." A hell-raiser is "energetic."

Edwin Newman, in his book *Strictly Speaking,* shows sadness at the abuse of the English language, especially by politicians and journalists, who specialize in noising their words abroad. He wrote of the excessive use and misuse of such words as *viable, activity,* and *situation.* A politician does not say there is "no alternative," but "no viable alternative." A weather man no longer predicts showers or thunderstorms but "shower activity" and "thunderstorm activity." Psychologists have difficulty speaking of children playing, they prefer children "in a play situation," and they feel important saying that children have not mastered "the reading situation."

This poor state of the language in the United States is not at the heart of our problem, Newman said, but it isn't divorced from it either. "It is at least conceivable that our politics would be improved if our English were, and so would other parts of our national life. If we were more careful about what we say, and how, we might be more critical and less gullible. Those for whom words have lost their value are likely to find that ideas have also lost their value."

Gobbledygook has been getting fun poked at it more than usual of late. When writing about advertising jargon, Nancy Stahl said in her newspaper column that if something is advertised as "improved," that means some of the most obvious faults have been eliminated. "All purpose" means it does a mediocre job on several things. "Time honored" means that so far we have won all the law suits brought against this product. "Hand crafted" means one leg is shorter than the others. "Exotic" is something that smells funny.

Washington columnist James J. Kilpatrick wrote about the jargon that fogged the air when President Ford's economic advisors met in October 1974. Here are a few sentences from the transcript:

> If you extrapolate the strains that we now already see as a consequence of what we have for an extended period of time, the institutions—economic, financial, structural—begin to break down because they are essentially constructed or have been developed over the decades in the context of low, single-digit inflation, and it's by no means clear or had not been clear, I should say, how significant this element was until we actually have tested it, and having tested it, we found that it does not respond terribly well.
>
> Clearly we see—I don't have to go through examples, I'm sure that all of you are most familiar with all of the various problems that each and every institution is having, but that clearly the sav-

ings and loans are under extraordinary pressure; insurance com-
panies, banks, business—especially smaller business—were having difficulty getting financing.
The system clearly does not work well under these conditions.

The only thing clear is that the speaker used the words *clear*
twice and *clearly* three times. The final sentence is the only one
that sounds like a human being speaking to human beings. No
wonder economics is called "the dismal science."

There are two sorts of obscurity in professional writing, one
negligent and one willful. Professionals often write with negli-
gence because they have not thought out what they want to say
and they have not learned to rewrite, the most difficult skill in
writing. Others burden their sentences with willful heaviness,
making sure that all felicity is banned, hoping that vagueness
reflects profundity. In both instances commonplace notions are
often sufficiently blurred to fool the unwary into feeling that
great meaning must be hidden beneath the rubble.

The professional's carefully acquired separateness, the
show of expertise, is a form of pride. He needs to return to
innocence to see his material with a fresh eye instead of
through the cluttered clichés of his trade.

There is this tendency for everyone going into any depth to
lose the grace of simplicity. Even when the material is subtle
and deep it can be subtle and deep in a direct way and not in an
esoteric, foggy way. The level of difficulty in comprehension
should be set by the level of difficulty in the thought, and not
by a confusion of words. William James, who certainly went
below the surface of things, always wrote with grace and
clarity—no sentence was more difficult than it need be.

Gobbledygook is always the result when writing is done for
the wrong reason. The right reason is the great desire to get
through to another human being. As Stendahl wrote to Balzac,
"I see but one rule: to be clear. If I am not clear, all my world
crumbles to nothing."

A politician might say his world would crumble to nothing if he is clear too often. When asked a question he would rather not answer, the politician uses the tactic of the cuttlefish, which emits ink, not to enlighten, but to confuse. On the eve of election, a governor, asked his opinion on Vietnam, said, "I think that our actions have not kept pace with the changing conditions, and therefore our actions are not completely relevant today to the realities of the magnitude and the complexity of the problems that we face in that conflict." A reporter asked, "Governor, what does that mean?" and the reply was, "Just what I said."

Sometimes gobbledygook is written as self-promotion. When a bureaucrat asked his secretary what she thought of a report he had just completed on juvenile delinquency, she said, "I think it is hard to read." He said, "It ought to be hard to read, I worked hard compiling it."

The word *compiling* was a fitting one because most gobbledygook is not written but compiled. It accumulates like hash. I learned this during World War II when for a year I served in the dangerous duty of writing military manuals. When working with old-line army officers I learned the secret for heavy-handed prose. They would write a sentence that was fairly decent, and then instead of spending the morning, as professional writers do, making it more lean and clear, they would spend the morning adding accretions, like barnacles on the bottom of a boat.

I was expected to do the same. The only way I could bring it off was to write sentences in fairly decent English and then translate them into military prose. To help in translation I made a list of rules that went something like this: Never write a simple sentence if you can twist and turn it into a compound complex sentence. Avoid the active voice in favor of the passive voice. Never say *first* when you can say *initial;* never use *end* when *terminate* is handy; never write *use* when *utilization* will do. *Inaugurate* is better than *start; compensate* is better than *pay;* and any five-syllable word is preferable to a one-syllable word meaning the same thing. Mix in words like *finalize, objectify, moreover,* and *heretofore,* just to add density to the texture. Anyone faced with a similar problem will find the following useful: *feasible, counterproductive, interdependent, multiphasic, outreach, supportative, implementations, interfaces, parameters.*

Whenever I was stuck with clarity I asked help from the fullest officer in the room and always received it, proving that style is the man, or as E. B. White said "Style is the self escaping into the open." It was in the army that I realized that writing is not about split infinitives, dangling participles, and the comma fault; it is an exercise in self-revelation, and if the self is dull then dullness is what escapes.

A theologian more than any army officers, politicians, physicians, and lawyers ought to search for simplicity, the price of which, according to Eliot, is everything. Through simplicity he helps others *see.* Ruskin said the greatest thing a human ever does in this world is to see something and tell what he saw in a plain way. He said, "Hundreds of people can talk for one who can think, and thousands can think for one who can see. To see clearly is poetry, prophecy and religion all in one."

A professional theologian with the highest credentials said, "A practical theology is needed, a theology that can be understood by the common man." And yet his own writing cannot be understood by the common man. Churchill said, "The short words are best, and the old words are best of all," and yet he too was sometimes guilty of purple passages. It is easy to preach this, but practicing it is another matter.

Both the theologian and Churchill, I feel sure, realized that it is not just what is said, but how it is said that is important. The what and the how interact to produce meaning. How an observation is made can thrill you with an insight or put you to sleep. Wonderful news burdened with jargon is polluted, but the same information presented with distinction may add something to life. Dehumanized writing builds barriers between sender and receiver; to use an expression from Martin Buber, it makes for an I-It rather than for an I-Thou relationship.

This then is a moral problem. Dag Hammarskjöld saw it as such when he wrote in *Markings:*

> Respect for the word is the first commandment in the discipline by which a man can be educated to maturity—intellectual, emotional and moral.
>
> Respect for the word—to employ it with scrupulous care and an incorruptible heartfelt love of truth—is essential if there is to be any growth in a society, or in the human race.
>
> To misuse the word is to show contempt for man. It undermines the bridges and poisons the wells. It causes Man to regress down the long path of evolution.

The theologian will need humility in this search for the kind of simplicity found in the best art and in the best morality. He will find that if he really works hard to make something clear many people will think that because it is clear there can't be much to it, and the more fancy among them will use the words "simplistic" and "reductionistic." Maybe there really won't be much to it, for clear writing reveals the vapid as surely as gobbledygook hides it. Yet even the vapid is best put clearly, for then it is out in the open and nobody is fooling anybody.

It is all too easy to fool people with a show of verbal fireworks, even people who have had much schooling. Especially people who have had much schooling. To prove this, three southern California educators, Dr. Donald H. Naftulin, John E. Ware, Jr., and Frank A. Donnelly, devised an experiment. They hired a professional actor and introduced him as Dr. Myron L. Fox, of Albert Einstein University. Before a group of psychiatrists, psychologists, and social workers all involved in education, the actor lectured on "A Mathematical Game Theory as Applied to Physical Education." He used academic jargon, double-talk, and strung one meaningless statement after another into a dreary string of gobbledygook. After the lecture the fifty-five educators who formed the audience were asked to fill out a questionnaire. Some of their comments: "Excellent presentation . . . enjoyed listening . . . has warm manner . . . good flow . . . seems enthusiastic . . . lively examples . . . extremely articulate . . . too intellectual." Not one of the educators realized his leg was being pulled. Practically all of them were convinced that they had learned something. The experiment indicated, said the men who staged it, that people are usually more satisfied with the illusion of having learned something than with really learning something.

For a theologian the most fitting approach to communication is the religious one shared by Franz Kafka, Dylan Thomas, and Dag Hammarskjöld. Kafka considered all sincere writing as a sacred expenditure of energy, an effort at communion with his fellow man. Dylan Thomas said he wrote poetry for the glory of God and would be a damned fool if he didn't. Hammarskjöld had a wonderful prayer of petition that he recorded in his journal: "Not to encumber the earth." If there is one thing gobbledygook does, it encumbers the earth. Like smog and sludge, and all forms of pollution, it is one more way of lowering life.

4: The Gospel
according to Today
as Found in the Mass Media

I was sensitized to seeing news in a new way while attending a production called *Something for Lent,* written by students at Immaculate Heart College in Los Angeles. The program said: "*Something for Lent* tries to take a look at the small and large pain of any and every person's daily life. Using some great words of great people and some ordinary words of ordinary people, we are trying to express the profound paradox of suffering most perfectly exemplified in Christ's passion. What we want to say is that each of us is responsible for alleviating pain wherever we find it and at the same time each of us is reborn only through suffering."

The students performed brief skits each telling about a different aspect of suffering. They used slides, films, tape recordings, newspaper want ads and radio commercials. They danced, sang, and carried posters and quoted Pope John, Carl Sandburg, James Joyce, Dostoevsky, Saint Paul, Ray Bradbury, and Jacques Maritain.

The program closed with a taped recording of news broadcast that evening from a Los Angeles radio station. Not just any evening, but of that *very* evening. By then members of the audience were so sensitized to suffering that they heard the

36

newscast in a whole new way, in a way they might continue to hear newscasts from that night on. A long sermon about the need for compassion could never make us feel compassion the way that presentation of concrete realities did. That will be ten years ago next Shrove Tuesday, but for me the effect still lingers.

I had a similar experience, a few years later, while attending the evening service for Trinity Sunday in the crypt of Saint Paul's Cathedral in London. In a large room, well designed even though it is deep underground, a group of young people from Liverpool presented a service in the round.

The program consisted of brief readings, songs, and dances, mostly contemporary, that were selected to develop the theme "Life and Growth," stressing the need for growth and the pain that accompanies it. Each of the sixteen segments dealt with contemporary communication to show the spiritual problems that come with being human in these times. Most members of the congregation were under thirty. Even those of us middle-aged or over had to admit that here was worship with dignity and reverence. Here was entertainment in a modern idiom that brought awareness of God's presence in the world.

If the main object of life is to worship God, then I suppose worship ought to saturate the day, even a day cluttered with mass communication. Dailiness as a spark for worship has good precedence: the psalmist used ordinary experience to lift the mind and heart to God; Aquinas urged everybody to see God everywhere in everything, and Meister Eckhart spoke of learning to pierce the veil of things to comprehend God within them.

Even a newspaper properly used can do something for the spirit, said Abbé Ernest Dimnet, but when badly used as scattered reading it hurries us along the path to becoming *evapores,* scatterbrains. When the abbé made that observation, in more quiet times, he could never have guessed how powerful and omnipresent the media were to become. The statistics for

United States alone would have appalled him: there are about 1,800 daily and 9,000 weekly newspapers, 20,000 magazines, 1,000 television and 7,000 radio stations; nearly 13,000 films are produced and 30,000 books published each year.

Such clamoring for attention! Not to let the clamor scatter the spirit is a problem. The media encourage inward dissipation, a tragedy in so many of our lives—watching television with apathy, scanning news columns out of boredom, and leafing through magazines with scattered attention.

To pay attention, to be collected, has become so much more difficult since Abbé Dimnet's time. An English spiritual director, Bernard Basset, S.J., used the expression, "the agnosticism of inattention," in his book *Let's Start Praying Again.* He said that an outright disbelief in God has been replaced by a turning to the trivial. So much time is given to *not* facing up to God. So often distractions are welcomed and life reduced to petty diversions, to something endured as a buzz and a blur and a vague sadness.

Father Basset agrees with Simone Weil that the quality of our attention counts much in the quality of our worship. In the mass media, he felt, the things that produce mindlessness are destructive, but anything that developes attention is worth pursuing:

> Personally, I exclude no program, documentary, educational, dramatic or bloody which stimulates my full attention and offers me a theme. Those programs are pernicious on television or on radio which have no theme, reach no catharsis and merely fragment the mind. Bursts of noise, snatches of music, weather reports, commercials, news headlines, gossip, all mixed together, cultivate inattention and make prayer impossible.

The mass media as a source of prayer is one of the sections in *Experiments in Prayer,* a book for young people by Betsy Caprio. She believes that something is really learned when it is learned from an experience that elicits both feeling and thinking, and so during her classes in religion she tries to bring young people an experience that teaches them to pray. For example, she asks the class to look through newspapers, to choose an item of interest from any section—it can be a story, an ad, a cartoon, a photograph—and use the item as a source of meditation.

One of her students observes that a war photograph indicates that God permits evil in the world. Another says that a home-run reminds him of man's need to use God-given talents. A third sees a wedding engagement as a reminder to pray for that couple's success in marriage.

Betsy Caprio has many ways to teach young people to see everything as a source of prayer. Someone draws a doodle and the class draws a prayer from it: a scribble of ovals evokes: "God, I'm going around in circles. Please straighten me out," and a scribble of a badly tangled piece of yarn brings forth, "Lord, sometimes I feel like I'm tied in a knot. When that happens please help me remember you."

If all of this sounds unsophisticated, remember the students are in their early teens. They are learning a way of seeing and listening that will mature as they do, and if it really catches on they will be reminded of God's presence in the world, almost in passing, by television commercials, billboards, songs, and anything else that comes along.

Religion and Personality is probably too sophisticated for most high school students, but in it Father Adrian van Kaam also agrees that an awareness of God ought to spring from the events of daily life. The priest-psychologist says that the mature religious personality breaks forth in spontaneous prayer from time to time daily, moved by an awareness of God in ordinary affairs, and that a well-balanced personality finds manifestations of goodness, truth, and beauty in daily life: "A sunset, a flower, a child, a poem may be thrilling and exciting, not once, but time and time again. The openness of the personality for reality leads to this ecstasy springing from the basic experiences of his life. He would not feel the same joy in winning sums of money, participating in a wild party, attend-

ing a cheap movie, or being praised for superficial pos-
sessions.'' Such a person is what Saint Augustine called, "an
alleluia from head to foot."

Let's take another look at this matter of finding an awareness of God in what Adrian van Kaam calls "ordinary affairs." The comic strip is a good one to consider because it is
an idiom developed in our time that seems an improbable
vehicle for spiritual insights. And yet a book, *The Gospel According to Peanuts,* by Robert Short shows what a serious
matter a comic strip can be.

That is because a Sunday school teacher, Charles Schultz,
who happens to be the creator of *Peanuts* believes that, "If
you do not say something in a cartoon you might as well not
draw it at all. Humor which does not say something is worth-
less humor." His characters say plenty. Several children and a
dog reflect the insights of Kierkegaard, Barth, Tillich, Newman, Salinger, and Eliot. It is unthinkable to put a crew of kids
up against such thinkers as Saint Paul, Isaias, and Shakespeare
and expect them to look good, but it works; through the genius
of Charles Schultz it works.

Peanuts can be taken on two levels, it can be enjoyed on the
surface level of children making funny remarks, or appreciated
at a deeper level when we observe them making perceptive
comments on life. To have insight into the deeper level one
needs to be aware of the writings and thought ranging from the
Scriptures to the existentialists.

It is amazing how much of a homily Schultz can crowd into
a four-panel strip. For example, one shows Snoopy, the
hound, shivering in the snow. Charlie Brown, well-bundled
against the elements, says, "Snoopy looks kind of cold,
doesn't he," and Linus, also well-bundled, answers, "I'll say
he does . . . maybe we ought to go over and comfort him."
Linus says, "Be of good cheer, Snoopy," and Charlie Brown
echoes, "Yes, be of good cheer," and both walk away leaving
Snoopy puzzled and still shivering in the snow.

Isn't that the Epistle of Saint James put into the idiom of our time? "If a brother or a sister be naked and destitute of daily food, and one of you say unto them, 'Depart in peace, be ye warmed and filled'; notwithstanding ye give them not those things which are needful to the body, what doth it profit?"

In his book *God Is More Present Than You Think,* Robert Ochs opens several chapters with quotations from the *Spiritual Exercises* of Ignatius, but two chapters open in a more contemporary way: one with a sequence from the comic strip *B.C.* and another with a few lines from a Shaw play.

In the comic strip, a character named B.C. is walking across an arid desert. He comes upon a stone signpost that says, "Duck!" He ducks and is narrowly missed by a flying brick.

The Shaw play, *St. Joan,* includes these telling lines:

Robert: How do you mean? Voices?
Joan: I heard voices telling me what to do. They came from God.
Robert: They came from your imagination.
Joan: Of course. That is how the messages of God come to us.

After reading the chapters we turn back to the comic strip and to the Shaw quotation and realize the theological implications in each. And, glory be, Father Ochs brought it off without debasing theology.

Turning stories into parables has a basis in tradition: the Scriptures are filled with anecdote. In recent years many theologians are seeing stories as a way to religious insight. They believe that the story approach might help more people than the strictly intellectual approach. Stories call not only on the mind but also on the intuitions, emotions, senses, and imagination. Most people are like Plutarch, who said that he did not so much understand matters through words as words through experience and knowledge of matters.

An experience may allow an insight to slip through the defenses at odd moments. The experience may be first-hand or

even one brought by the mass media. This is a kind of serendipity, a happy surprise, something we hadn't planned on.
Some of these insights caught on the wing may move us more
deeply than those consciously sought.

It is possible that something on television might indirectly
bring an awareness of the shortness of life in a way that the
psalms and Thomas à Kempis might not. Merv Griffin would
be surprised to hear that his show can be a source of meditation. While watching some of his guests one can't help but be
moved by an awareness of mortality. One night when George
Raft and Pat O'Brien were guests, film clips were shown of
Raft in the role of Steve Brodie and O'Brien as Father Duffy.
To see those men in their prime and as they are now must
move even an unthinking person to a moment of solemnity. It
brings to mind Dylan Thomas's sad and moving line, "I see
the boys of summer in their ruin."

A priest was talking about the problem of "listening," not a
matter of keeping the ears open, but of hearing the whole tone
of another person. He used as a simple example something he
"heard" through his eyes while watching a basketball game
between the United States and Russia on television! "I
watched a young Russian boy take a foul shot. I watched his
intentness. The mop of hair over his eyes. The play of muscles. And suddenly I said to myself, 'He might as well be an
American boy.' That is what I mean by listening. Listening to
the whole young man."

This may sound simple and evident, but it isn't, not really.
It is possible to go through life and miss the insight that gave
the young priest a new way of seeing people. He was probably
told time and again that he should see people that way, but
theory does not necessarily bring realization.

Just today I came across a sentence written by the Greek
poet Hesiod, three thousand years ago. He spoke of "a wind
so cold that it would take the hide off an ox." It was something
I might have heard a farmer say when I was a boy in Kentucky.

(Hesoid would have felt right at home to hear: ''The only way to get shed of wild onions is to die and leave them.'') It gave me a feeling of kinship with the distant past, an awareness that my roots are deep, and a sense of how unchanging people are, things worth being reminded of.

In a magazine, *Industrial Photography,* I saw a photograph, lovely in its cool sea greens and rich browns. It appeared to be a seascape in the South Pacific. Certainly, it was pleasing, until I read the lines beneath it: a photomicrograph of a ruby laser burn in the human retina. I flinched. The picture was less pleasing now. Here was a lesson in the poverty of my objectivity. I am a bundle of subjectivity, so influenced by past impressions that it's difficult to give something a fresh look, a fact worth facing.

These are simple examples, I know—the young priest watching a Russian on television, a homey expression of an ancient poet, and the picture of a laser burn in a magazine—but each brought a reminder of something worth being reminded of. All truths when realized seem embarrassingly simple. We tend to know things in our heads—but that is only half knowing—and then suddenly, presto, something happens and we realize some truth of life down into the crevices of the soul. That's knowing!

As we grow older, experience serves as a magnet to draw meaning from words and events, meaning that was there all along but we were not ready for it. A woman who had lived long enough to become aware of how time gets us ready for certain realizations said that everyone should read *War and Peace* three times: in youth for the story, in middle age for the history, and in old age for the philosophy and theology.

Father Basset read the *Confessions* of Saint Augustine six times and felt he did not really begin to comprehend the message until in his middle fifties. ''The words, the thoughts, the plan of the book have not altered throughout the centuries; I read the same sentences now that I read thirty years ago. The change is not in Augustine but in myself. The cold fact is that one begins to take religion seriously only when one is vividly aware of death. Where, in youth, death was a macabre threat to other and older people, it suddenly becomes in middle age a definite entry in one's engagement pad.''

Among the books on my shelves are some that I have begun reading time and again, getting nowhere because they seem alien to me. They fire no spark, make no contact with my inner life. Trying to read them is like trying to start a car on a cold morning. Then all of a sudden on a certain day I find the very book I could not read speaking to my new self. A shadow has passed from some inner corner of the psyche and I am ready for it.

As the years pass even contemporary events should be seen in a new light. The Abbé Dimnet was right, the news is filled with lessons for the soul. Even scandal can teach something, depending on how it is seen. Some scandal needs be reported in the news, but the trouble with reporting any of it is that the audience expects the second and the third acts of a scandal to live up to the first. The media might justify reporting the first act under the ''right of the people to know.'' The trouble is the people tend to want to know more than they have a right to and the media go along.

I was in London when two lords resigned their high positions in government when blackmailed by a call girl. That much could be published under the right of the people to know. The people clamored for more and got it. They got photographs of the girl's aunt, a mother superior of a convent in Ireland, and photographs of the girl's parents in Cork. When such innocent people are dragged into a scandal we ought to be aware that the media are giving a shabby performance. This awareness might discourage the voyeuristic leer and the smacking of lips and even lead to some compassion.

When men fall from high places, as did the two English lords, we have tragedy without the saving grace of an aesthetic experience. In time an artist may tell of these events in such a way as to lead an audience to compassion through an aesthetic experience, but in the meanwhile we have to hunt for compassion on our own.

Scandal can have a sobering effect if for no other reason than that it is a reminder that going through life is like crossing a mined field, the next step can maim or destroy. If such things happen to others they can happen to us. Of a certain scandal an Irish girl said in a radio interview, "I guess the whole truth about any one of us would shock all the rest of us."

This sounds as though I discount moral judgment. It is not moral judgment but moral indignation that spoils things. Indignation makes reformers unpleasant to have around. It makes them the enemies of their own causes because it makes the "right" they stand for so unattractive. Wild-eyed Democrats and wild-eyed Republicans each drive me out of the house. Fierce Catholics make me want to turn to Mohammedanism, or any other religion, but, of course, every religion has enough zealots to make their side of the fence equally unattractive. The axe-grinders, hard-sellers, arm-twisters distort life and drain serenity from it. I find it harder to feel compassion for them than for those involved in scandal.

While handing out compassion, in our survey of the day's news, let's not forget those who have attracted the media's fierce attention. In covering two national political conventions I was so aware of the barbarity of what is called aggressive news coverage that it made me ashamed of my craft. While watching the evening news on television, the sight of newsmen attacking political figures with microphones, cameras, and questions must make anyone of substance think twice before entering political life. In the nineteenth century many American Indians avoided photographers out of fear that their spirits might be stolen by the camera's eye. What seemed a superstition was really a perceptive intuition. Too much publicity, too much invasion of privacy, surely must damage the inner life.

Newspapers and newscasts are filled with lessons in what old-fashioned spiritual directors used to call "the inordinate attachment to things." Tonight's news speaks parables of such inordinate attachment—the energy shortage, war, pollution. Inordinate attachment is a specialty of many advertisements and commercials. The advertiser used to try to. make us want something we lacked, a car, a refrigerator, a TV set, but now that we have all those things he tries to make us dissatisfied with the brand we have. In recent years he even goes so far as to attack the competitor's brand, showing how it lacks the virtues of his own product.

Some attitudes revealed in advertisements are less than lovely. A current commercial, for instance, shows how satisfying it is to make other people jealous. A man struts from his house glorying in the sight of the neighbors eating their hearts out as he gets into his new car. Just being aware of wrong-headedness when found in the media can have a strengthening effect. It brings to mind the high school English teacher who tells her students that whenever they hear someone make a mistake in grammar they should silently correct it in their own minds and in so doing strengthen their right use of the language.

After all of this talk about how the mass media can be used for inner growth, I feel uneasy admitting that in the morning I tend to avoid newspapers, magazines, radio, and television. They set the wrong mood for the day. Journalists work on the proposition that things are expected to go right and so news by its nature is bad. Since happiness is seldom considered newsworthy, all journalism needs be approached with the resignation that the shadowy side of the spirit gets more air-time and larger headlines than the bright side. Newspapers and newscasts are not passports to serenity. The front page is designed to make one groan, and the anchorman's offerings feature anguish.

Dreary news can inspire a prayer even at dawn, of course it

can, but I don't relish starting the day that way. It is true, though, that what is one man's despair can be another's thanksgiving. For example, a friend of mine finds that listening to the traffic reports on radio while shaving leads to an act of thanksgiving. When cars are stacked up from the detour to infinity and the policeman in the helicopter speaks of "bumper-to-bumper," and "fender-bender," and "spin-out," my friend is grateful that he is within walking distance of his work: A prayer of thanksgiving from the bottom of the heart!

Such prayers of serendipity, such happy surprises, blend the sacred and the secular. They spare you the schizophrenia of filing the spiritual in one compartment and the management of affairs in another.

I find the early hours too precious, though, to give to the news. It is then that the ideas, thoughts and intuitions, inhabiting the warren below the surface of consciousness, are enticed into the open more readily than later, when the day gets shabby at the edges. The early hours, like the early years of life, set a tone and give a shape that tends to endure. The mood of life it seems is created more through little things than through big events. Walt Whitman must have been thinking of this when he wrote:

There was a child went forth every day,
And the first object he look'd upon, that object he became;
And that object became part of him for the day or a certain part
   of the day,
Or for many years, or stretching cycles of years.

The classics set a suitable tone for the day, one that suits me. They move with dignity and bring the consolation that nothing important is really new: Life goes on in spite of everything, and man does endure. They stretch time beyond our allotted years, offering a more copious life, a richness worth sensing at the start of a day.

Plutarch, with his lofty view of what it means to be a man, is a good morning companion. It is not surprising that in the eleventh century, nine hundred years after Plutarch's death, a bishop still held him in such affection that he prayed, "If, Lord, thou are willing in thy grace to save any Pagans from the wrath of God, I pray thee humbly to save Plato and Plutarch."

Plutarch's soul shows in something he wrote at the time of his daughter's death. "We are to think [of the dead] that they pass to a better place and a happier condition. Let us behave ourselves accordingly, outwardly by an ordered life, while within all should be pure, wise, incorruptible. . . . Is God so petty, so attached to the trifling, that He will take the trouble to create souls if we have nothing divine in us, nothing that resembles Him, nothing lasting or sure, but all of us fades like a leaf?"

The classics help us say "Yes" to life because they help us realize that ancient wisdom is still wise. When men of the past speak to our condition they console us with the realization that we are all in the same boat with no need to feel alone. The classics teach—at least this is what they teach me—that patterns of human behavior have not changed any more than the law of gravity.

The ancients give me pride in discovering I know things without knowing I know them. Deep calls to deep and something shimmers to the surface and I find myself articulating a point of view that has been lying there unformed, a hidden hunch. It is thrilling to find that someone living centuries ago saw life much as you do. I know how Dom Bede Griffiths felt when he first encountered Marcus Aurelius in the *Meditations:*

> I shall never forget how the "piety" of Marcus Aurelius touched me, his deep reverence for nature and for the order of the universe, which he expressed in the words, "Shall one say of Athens, O beautiful City of Cecrops, and shall not I say of the world, O beautiful City of God?" His conception of nature as one vast organism in which each element had to play its part and in which

each individual human life was but one element, appealed both to my imagination and my reason. It offered an explanation of the problem of evil, which was closely akin to that of Spinoza, that the cause of suffering was that each individual could not see his place in the pattern of the whole and thereby put himself in conflict with it; but if he could learn by reason to know his place within the whole, and deliberately accept it, then though he might suffer in his feelings his mind would be at peace. No less appealing was the idea that virtue was not something which required a reward, but that it was its own reward. To be virtuous was to live according to the reason, the law of the universe, of which our own reason was a part, and a virtuous act was simply an action which was "according to nature" like the growth of fruit on a tree. (*The Golden String*, p. 50)

The morning news rarely gives such a bright direction to the day as the dialogue that Plato put into the mouths of Socrates and Ion. They speak of how the Divinity intervenes in daily matters, explaining how man draws power from the Divine Magnet, another way of saying everybody steals from God. This awareness of God's intervention is at such a low ebb right now that the expression "a godsend," often used by our forefathers, is seldom heard any more. To be reminded that there is such thing as "a godsend" makes the day seem worth starting.

The classics at dawn can even prepare one for the commercials on the six o'clock news. Something Marcus Aurelius wrote nearly two thousand years ago could be used on the Walter Cronkite show, another reminder of how little life changes:

Are you irritated with one whose arm-pits smell? Are you angry with one whose mouth has a foul odor? What good will your anger do you? He has this mouth; he has these arm-pits. Such emanations must come from such things. "But the man has reason," you will say, "and he could, if he took pains, discover wherein he offends." I wish you well of your discovery. Now that you too have reason, by your rational faculty, stir up his rational faculty. Show him his fault. Admonish him.

An early morning awareness of the past helps bring some balance to the evening news. We have to supply the balance because newscasters do not specialize in the long view. We see the evening news in a different light if Herodotus has reminded us at dawn that, ''The cities which were formerly great have most of them become insignificant. And such as are at present powerful were weak in olden time. I shall, therefore, discourse equally of both, convinced that human happiness never continues long in one stay.''

An hour in the library looking through old newspapers and outdated magazines does something for the perspective. You notice that they reflect the energies of their time, energies that seemed important then but are no longer ours. The specific preoccupations and detailed interests of one generation can puzzle the next. So many concerns are as fading as fads.

And yet the basics endure—good and evil, life and death, love and hate. Sometimes while reading a newspaper I feel that here is a story I wrote as a young reporter thirty-five years ago and that only the names and addresses have been changed. André Gide wrote in his journal, ''Everything, now, seems to be a repetition'' and ''The same anew'' is the way James Joyce put it. As someone scribbled on a wall in an English village: ''The world ended yesterday. Today is an instant replay.''

Once you notice the repetition of things you begin to see life as a carousel. If you stand right here watching the spotted horse disappear off to the right, you know that if you are around long enough he will loom up over there to the left and come past again. After seeing this happen enough you get the feeling of here-is-where-I-came-in. Your response to that feeling tells what you are at the core, because as you grow older you become more completely what you have been all along. You may end up crochety, full of burrs and barbed wire, or serene in your amusement at the sight of all that over-reaching and fireworks.

Alice Roosevelt Longworth, who has seen more than her share of the hoopla featured in the mass media, has learned to take it in stride, judging from something she said on her ninetieth birthday. Asked what is the main difference between being ninety and nineteen, she said, "At ninety you are more amused."

She would have been amused at the headline in the local paper last December 31—Troubled World Awaits New Year's Revelry. She knows that the same headline would have been fitting on any December 31 in the past and that if the printer holds the type it could rightly be used on any New Year's Eve in the future. And for some reason that is amusing, if you are old enough and have not let the mass media spoil your life.

5: Films Can Offer More than Meets the Eye

I had just finished giving a talk at the national meeting of Diocesan Liturgical Commissions when a gaunt young man came to the podium. He introduced himself as a Trappist from the Abbey of Gethsemani, in Kentucky. The Trappists, he said, have been using books for centuries as a source of spiritual growth, and now they wonder if they ought not use films, too. Would I come to the monastery to talk about this? Don't try to sell the idea. Just talk about it and the monks will make up their own minds.

That is how I happened to screen films and give three lectures in the long narrow chapter room at the Abbey of Gethsemani. Monks in white robes, with black scapulars and cowls, sat on tiered benches along the walls and on chairs in the center. My first thought was that this is an improbable place to show films. Usually I feel anachronistic trying to cope with the present, but in the great chapter hall I felt like a man of the present thrust into the past.

I began by speaking of the advantages of supplementing philosophy and theology with literature and films in a search for truth, a search to realize "what God hath wrought." Through the storyteller, man must find himself, said Ivo Andric in accepting the Nobel Prize for Literature.

I think what he meant was that in accepting someone's

realization full-blown as it is offered in philosophy and theology you have not paid the price for it. You have to work your way through to that realization. That is the price. In realizing some truth of life through a novel, a play, or a film, you are helped to it through the particular incidents, in particular lives, bit by bit, paying the price as you go by reaching the insight gradually. The effect this way is quite different from reaching the insight through abstraction. Philosophy and theology tend to keep the realization above the eyebrows, but the story thrusts it into the marrow of the whole being.

In Bernard Malamud's novel *The Assistant*, a boy and a girl meet in the neighborhood library. He asks her what she is reading.

"*The Idiot*. Do you know it?"

"No. What's it about?"

"It's a novel."

"I'd rather read the truth."

"It is the truth."

Malamud makes this statement in another way in his play *Suppose a Wedding*. A retired Yiddish actor, Feuer, tangles with a young man who can only speak of tragedy in terms of Aristotle's theory of catharsis. Feuer says, "Don't quote me your college books. A writer writes tragedy so people don't forget they are human. He shows us the conditions that exist. He organizes us for the meaning of our lives so it is clear to our eyes. That's why he writes it, that's why we play it."

When a new work of fiction speaks of these deep matters of the heart, whether the medium be a play, a novel, or a film, the same theme was probably explored by the Greek and Elizabethan dramatists and the nineteenth-century novelists. All art rebuilds with the same old blocks, reinterprets the same ruins, in fresh and interesting ways.

I think I know what Thornton Wilder meant when he said, "Literature is the orchestration of platitudes." In reading the classics and the latest of the contemporary he could scarcely help but come to that conclusion. All the great human themes have been reported on—the need to love and to be loved, the pain of change, the sureness of decay, the yearning for something above and beyond self, and similar bits and pieces of the human mosaic. An old professor of the classics was so aware of these repeating themes that each semester he reminded his students that "Every great work was written this morning." If literature is "What oft was said, but ne'er so well express'd" that is what the great films are, too.

Since such awareness of the human spirit is a religious concern, films are now used in religious education. By religious education I mean anything that is done to enlarge and sensitize the spirit. Such education helps the spirit care about what lifts life and feel repelled by what lowers life. With this broad definition, religious education can include personal meditation, a religious retreat, CCD classes, a Sunday homily, a series of Lenten sermons, and a course in a classroom. In religious education, films can sensitize you to God's creation, bring insights into the human condition, and motivate a discussion.

I told the Trappists how the film *The Hat,* an eighteen-minute animation, was used to motivate a discussion on one of the religious programs produced by the Columbia Broadcasting System. The producer of the program asked a bishop, a rabbi, and a minister to attend the screening and to spend the remaining forty minutes of the hour speaking the thoughts that the brief film had brought to mind. The three men were wise in their talk about the problem of selfishness in the world, which is what the film is about.

If the producer had not screened the film but had asked them to go right ahead and start talking about selfishness, the conversation may not have been so effective. It would have been less definite. The three were motivated in their discussion by something definite on the screen. It set the tone, it set their feet on the ground. Too often in discussions, glittering generality follows glittering generality, until just a dull drone passes through one ear and out the other, leaving nothing on the spirit except the gray dust of ennui.

Generalities and abstractions have a place in such discussions, but they ought to spring from specifics, because life is lived as one definite experience after another. We live and grow mainly through the facts of events and arrive at abstract insights through them. I often recall an old Jew who upon hearing an abstract principle used to say, "Give me a for instance." The speaker would then say, "For instance..." and give a concrete example from which the old man would see through to the abstract conclusion. Films are "for instances" that lead to abstract insights and observations.

Another tendency is to let outward things stay outward and never become inward, especially if the outward is something not taken seriously, as is often the case with films. To keep the outward and the inward separate is disturbing to anyone who has a feeling for the prayer in Plato's *Phaedrus:* "Let the outward and the inward man become as one."

Frederick von Hugel, the theologian, did not mention films in his list of things that can help the soul advance, but they do fit his pattern of thought: "No soul can really advance just simply by itself; either books, or letters, or pictures, or the words or actions of others are, sooner or later, and more or less always necessary, always indeed operative within us, for good or for evil, or for both."

When that sentence was written, early in this century, films were mainly for entertainment and seldom grappled with problems of the spirit in more than some shallow and sentimental way. Even now only a small percentage of films produced can be used for spiritual insight. That can be said of books, too.

In film, as in the mass media, the thing that touches the spirit and brings an insight often comes as serendipity. That a certain film is considered religious might come as a surprise to all concerned. The producers of *The Hat* never expected that it would be nationally televised on a religious program. A priest said that when he saw, *The Heart Is a Lonely Hunter* he came away feeling that it had done more for him than a spiritual retreat, an admission he made with some embarrassment because things are not supposed to happen that way. Martha Graham would have been surprised to hear a nun tell me that everything Miss Graham says in *A Dancer's World* can just as readily be said about nuns.

I was surprised enough by that observation to book the film, and sure enough, everything said in it is also true of Trappists, surgeons, writers, and all human beings who strive to do something well enough to lift life. It doesn't make any difference if that something is physical, mental or spiritual, the basic rules for earning a superb performance are always the same.

In the opening minutes of this lecture-demonstration, Martha Graham explains how a dancer feels just before a performance. "There's a moment of dread, a sense of hazard, a feeling that perhaps you haven't done quite enough work. Perhaps you should go back to the studio and work again because that which you do not want to do is to fail in either clarity or passion. You have given all of your life to doing one thing. It sounds grim, it sounds frightening. It isn't. It has a great gaiety at times and a great wonder. But at the same time there is that need to go back to the studio."

The word studio could be changed to novitiate, if Miss Graham were talking about nuns, or changed to medical school if she were talking about surgeons. The word studio as she uses it does not stand for a place so much as for an attitude: the willingness to accept discipline and dedication for the sake of enhancing life.

Only discipline and dedication can give a dancer, or anyone else, the freedom to rise above mediocrity. As Miss Graham says, "The dancer is a realist. His craft teaches him to be. Either the foot is pointed or it is not and no amount of dreaming will point it.

"This requires discipline, not drill. Not something imposed

from without, but discipline imposed by you yourself upon yourself. Your goal is freedom, but freedom may only be achieved through discipline. In the studio you learn to conform, to submit yourself to the demands of your craft so that you may finally be free.''

Spontaneity, a word much abused by those who don't want the pressures of discipline and dedication, is something else that Miss Graham explains. As it applies to the dancer, she says: "It takes time. It takes about ten years of study. Someone said that everyone is born a genius but that some people only keep it a few minutes. In other words, what happens when you have to work ten years? You get tired. But those who press through finally arrive at a moment when they don't have to dance in groups of forty or fourteen. They become one of four. Or even one. They are really individuals now. They have reached the full maturity in their craft. At last they have spontaneity. Now they can make everything they do seem as though it is being done for the first time. They have reached clarity.''

A Dancer's World has some excellent performances, beautiful bodies moving beautifully through space. The film's greatest value, though, is that it lets the audience catch a glimpse of the beautiful character of Martha Graham. She has a reverence for life. She holds it with such consecration that she cannot clutter it up with inadequacies. She is dedicated to lifting life. She is an ascetic in the best sense of the word; her austerities grow out of her life naturally, making it a unity, for life is best lived as a unified whole, as a work of art.

If films are used as part of a course, they might well be selected to develop certain themes, for this helps give structure to a course, some insurance against churning up chaos. The by-product of any course might well be some sense of plan.

The Commandments, for example, could be the theme for a film series. The commandment that admonishes, ''Thou shalt not have strange gods before you,'' can be illustrated by *The*

River, which tells of the worship of the strange gods, greed and avarice. *The River,* a classic documentary made in 1937, shows that when man abuses the land, out of greed, he pays the price of impoverishment. It shows how he cut down the trees and planted badly until the soil eroded and when the rains came, the floods followed and drowned the towns. It dramatizes the ways we have abused our gifts until we are left with an impoverished abundance.

The River tells of a lack of reverence—there is no fear of the Lord, in the sense used in the later Hebrew Scriptures, in the sense of humility and awe: "The fear of the Lord is the crown of wisdom, it makes peace and health to flourish."

The River is imbued with a sense of *hubris.* The ancient Greeks believed in *hubris,* the pride that precedes the fall. They believed that arrogance carries the seeds of its own destruction. *Hubris* in Christian terms might be that "he who thinks he stands must take heed lest he fall."

The arrogance that destroys what God gave us always leaves us with a price to pay. So a screening of *The River* can tie together several things: a teaching of the ancient Hebrews, "Thou shalt not have strange gods before you," and an insight of the ancient Greeks, *hubris,* and a problem of modern Americans, the impoverishment of the land. This can bring the realization that teachings of long ago are worth attending to even now. We need frequent reminders that some things worth remembering were said before last Tuesday, an observation that the Trappists approved of.

The commandment "Thou shalt not kill" could motivate the screening of *The Great Holiday Massacre,* a CBS documentary produced by Edward R. Murrow and Fred Friendly a dozen years ago, but what it says grows more true each year. It tells of the modern American's favorite murder weapon—the automobile. With it he kills 56,000 people a year and maims about 400,000 more, some so badly that they would be better off dead.

This brings to mind a modern parable: The God of Progress appeared before the Premier of a new African state and said, "I will give you a great network of superhighways, if—"

"If what?" asked the Premier.

"If you will sacrifice 28,000 of your citizens to me."

"Of course not! What a horrible suggestion," cried the Premier.

"What's so horrible," asked the God of Progress. "The United States pays me a tribute of twice that *every year*."

The excessive use of the automobile kills in ways not tabulated in the safety statistics. How much it kills by polluting the air with exhaust is unknown. How much it destroys all kinds of resources and energies cannot be accurately measured. The automobile kills our heritage, too. It has a way of erasing the past that not even war can rival. It causes old landmarks to be torn down, bulldozed over, and capped with cement and blacktop. It covers over history and makes rootlessness a way of life. All sense of place is being destroyed, turned into Nowhere. As Joni Mitchell says in one of her songs, we are making a parking lot out of Paradise. So many scenes in *The Great Holiday Massacre* are as surrealistic as a parking lot because the approach to each American city has become surrealism. All of this new harshness must make for a harshness of spirit.

The Great Holiday Massacre as much as *The River* brings the insight that all excess carries a built-in retribution, for excessiveness is somehow a form of arrogance, a part of *hubris*. In an essay printed in *Great Essays in Science* Thomas Henry Huxley wrote of this in a picturable way. He said that each of us is playing a game of chess and that the way we play it has something to do with our own happiness and to some extent with the happiness of others:

> The chess board is the world, the pieces are the phenomena of the universe, the rules of the game are what we call the laws of Nature. The player on the other side is hidden from us. We know

that his play is always fair, just and patient. But also we know, to our cost, that he never overlooks a mistake, or makes the smallest allowance for ignorance. To the man who plays well, the highest stakes are paid, with the sort of overflowing generosity with which the strong shows delight in strength. And one who plays ill is checkmated—without haste, but without remorse.

Maybe Huxley never thought of it that way, but what he is speaking of is the virtue of temperance, the right and orderly use of created things. *The Great Holiday Massacre* and *The River* speak of intemperance, the wrong and disorderly use of created things. Other films that show how intemperance brings on the checkmate "without haste, but without remorse" are those about pollution, alcoholism, smoking, drug addiction. All of these have to do with people who haven't been listening, listening to learn the rules of the game. They were too arrogant. In *The Circle,* a documentary about drug addicts who are trying to help each other, the addicts themselves make the point, again and again, that they never listened. In their long, violent sessions with each other they come to realize that they can defy parents, police, president, and pope and perhaps get by with it, but once they defy Nature they are checkmated, sometimes even with haste. They are learning to listen, which is as much a part of communication as learning to send.

Another theme worth exploring in films would be some dramatic sentence from Scripture. For example, the one Saint Paul wrote to the Corinthians: "If someone must brag, let him brag about the Lord." Any film that stands in awe of creation brags about the Lord. Many science films, especially those made with some poetic insight, are hymns of praise for the wonders that God has wrought. They bring the realization that science is revelation in our time.

What a natural way for us living in a scientific age to learn about God. The proper study of any creator is his created work, whether the creator be Wordsworth, Eliot, Auden, or God. The highest praise anyone can give any creator is to appreciate his work. Just to be definite about this, let's take as examples two short films, *Overture/Nyitany* and *Cosmic Zoom,* both scientifically accurate and aglow with poetic insight.

Overture/Nyitany reveals the splendor of new life. The camera through x-ray photography shows the growth of a chicken inside an egg. The sound track is filled with a symphony. As the chicken fights through its shell and finally stands free, the music builds to a climax. The audience feels like cheering. Here an artist does what an artist is supposed to do—show the importance of things. His job is to show how very unusual is the usual in the world as God made it.

Cosmic Zoom makes you feel both very small and very great. Small because you are such a speck in all of this cosmos; great because you are a part of this exciting universe. The film opens with a boy rowing on the river. The camera does a breath-taking zoom away from him until he is just a speck. Then the river is a speck. The continent is a speck. We zoom back and back and up and up into space, flashing past patterns of heavenly bodies, witnessing galaxies of beautiful design. Suddenly the camera pauses. We begin a hectic return through space, zooming in until once more we focus on the boy in the boat. The camera takes us to a close-up of his hand where a mosquito is perched. It zooms into the proboscis of the mosquito, on into the blood it is sucking and deep into the patterns that are remarkably similar to the ones seen in outer space. Again the camera stops and comes zooming back, hurtling us through a return journey of innerspace. Finally we are back to a medium shot of the boy in the boat and he goes rowing down the river. We are a little breathless at all the extraordinary things happening in less time than it takes to make one stroke with an oar in the river. It brings a flicker of awareness of the complexity and the simplicity of the present moment.

During the first session, I screened for the Trappists

Overture/Nyitany and *Cosmic Zoom*. By coincidence, when the monks gathered for prayer at 3:15 the next morning they chanted Psalm 18, the one about the heavens proclaiming the Glory of God. During the next lecture I said that I hoped Psalm 18 now meant more to them after having seen those films. The nods of assent throughout the chapter hall indicated that for some monks the films brought that psalm up to date, made it more real for today, and helped them realize how science can be revelation in our time.

Films can also be used to stretch concepts that have shrunken in popular use. The concepts of death and love, for example, are narrowly held. To stretch the concepts of these two great truths is important because the spirit is influenced by the way death and love are seen.

The popular concept of death is that it is something recorded in an obituary column, a concept that needs to be stretched until one sees that death comes to everyone long before the notice gets into the papers. This concept could be developed in a course on the theology of death by screening several feature films: *Death of a Salesman* tells of the death of false dreams and the death of a certain way of life. In *The Seventh Seal* a man tries to catch up with God before Death catches up with him. In *Ikuru* a man given six months to live tries to find a life worth living. *Requiem for a Heavyweight* tells of the death of a career. In *Umberto D* an old man suffers the death of his spirit.

As for the short films, *Anytime* and *Please Don't Count the Candles,* both documentaries, make painfully clear the death that precedes death when people feel they have outlived their usefulness. *Wilf* describes the death of a way of life. All of these make us aware that things keep changing, and life is a succession of views, and death stands by in many forms.

To be more specific about this idea of the omnipresence of death, let's look in some detail at *The House*. This half-hour film, made in the Netherlands, presents memories of an old house that is being torn down. The scenes of destruction are intercut with glimpses of lives lived within those walls through two generations. The memories are presented, not in chronological order, but in a thoroughly shuffled jumble, the way memories recur. The theme, filled with intimations of mortality, speaks of construction and destruction, rise and fall. The downfall of things is shown in several ways: the house is built and torn down; people are born, grow old, and die; there is a moral decline and a decline of a culture.

The House brings the awareness that everything that the eye falls upon is dying. The old man in the rocker is dying, yes, but the rocker is dying, too. Everything suffers the terminal flaw of impermanence. There is a brotherhood between the animate and the inanimate, so that there really are sermons in stones. This can lead to some understanding of Francis of Assisi's mystical insight when he not only addressed human beings as brother, but also spoke of Brother Wolf and Brother Fire.

I spoke earlier about using the classics and the mass media to help us realize how the past and the present flow together. *The House* makes the same observation that Heraclitus made five hundred years before Christ when he said that nothing endures but change. He said to his wife, "Time is like a river which is flowing endlessly through the universe, and you can't step in the same river twice, Helen."

Long before that, fifteen hundred years and more before Homer, the Sumerian *Epic of Gilgamesh* speaks to the same condition that Heraclitus and *The House* speak to: "There is no permanence. Do we build a house to stand forever, do we seal a contract to hold for all time? Do brothers divide an inheritance to keep forever, does the flood-time of rivers endure? From the days of old there is no permanence. The sleeping and the dead, how alike they are. What is there between the master and the servant when both have fulfilled their doom?"

So here is a case of an ancient manuscript and a modern film showing a kinship that helps us feel related to everybody alive and to everybody who ever lived. This is communication, humanity speaking to humanity, bringing into our lives a certain gravity and awe that is a form of worship.

All of this leads to the realization of the pain of change. This is the theme of *Goodnight, Socrates,* a short film about a Greek neighborhood that was torn down in Chicago to make way for a superhighway. The pain that this change brought to one family is rendered so poignantly that an old priest identifying with it said to me, "You ought to show that to more people. Then they will understand how some of us feel about the changing Church."

The concept of love is even more narrowly held than that of death. A course in the theology of love could use films to develop in some detail a paragraph in Rollo May's book *Love and Will:*

> There are four kinds of love in Western tradition. One is *sex,* or what we call lust, libido. The second is *eros,* the drive of love to procreate or create—the urge, as the Greeks put it, toward higher forms of being and relationship. A third is *philia,* or friendship, brotherly love. The fourth is *agape* or *caritas* as the Latins called it, the love which is devoted to the welfare of the other, the prototype of which is the love of God for man. Every human experience of authentic love is a blending, in varying proportions, of these four.

The course in the theology of love might be developed around a series of short films: *The Quiet One* tells of a Harlem boy's need to be loved. *String Bean* tells of an old woman's need to love, even if the object is only a bean plant. *Cross Country Runner* brings the realization of how the love of getting ahead in life can kill all other kinds of love. *A Light for John,* never filed under the category of a love story, really is a love story, a documentary that shows the mutual love (*agape* or *caritas*) of an old woman and her middle-aged mentally retarded son. This list could be extended to dozens of films to serve as a start for discussions that stretch the concept of love. The way we see love and death give us away for what we are.

Not one of the films mentioned so far will be filed in a catalog under the heading of Religion. Even the people who made them would be surprised to hear that I suggested the Trappists look at them. When using films, as when using books, it is best not to be too much of a slave to the catalog listing. Look at them and see them for what they are.

Films that will be filed under Religion in a catalog are made at the Franciscan Communications Center in Los Angeles. In the past ten years some remarkably good short subjects have come from there.

The Stray, for example, is a fifteen-minute delight that has enough universality of appeal to please nearly everyone from kindergarten to the nursing home. The story is about a bus driver who takes a dozen children to the zoo. One, of course, gets lost. As you may have guessed, this is the parable of the Good Shepherd retold in a modern idiom. If I were a pastor, on the Sunday that the story of the Good Shepherd appears in the Gospel I would be tempted to screen *The Stray* right there in front of God and everybody. I can't imagine a fifteen-minute sermon that will make the point as well as that film.

William, another Franciscan film, is something of a modern parable. An eight-year-old boy, clumsy and shy, doesn't fit in at a gigantic picnic where everyone seems busy being assertive and selfish, eating too much and playing too hard. William has enough inner resources to enjoy exploring a small woods near the picnic grounds, where he finds pleasure in turtles, worms, crickets and birds. When he returns to the picnic everyone is on the ground feverishly searching for something. Not knowing what they are looking for, William picks up a snail and under it finds a piece of jewelry; his gift of awe and wonder has led him to "the pearl of great price." Having been shunned all day he is now treated as a hero because he has found what everyone else has been looking for. The film ends with William facing a decision—now that he is accepted should he go along with the crowd or keep his individuality.

The Franciscans showed perception when they developed sixty-second films, called telespots, that use the format of a television commercial. They showed a sense of communication in realizing that the people they want to reach are accustomed to receiving their attitudes packaged in this format.

Man as producer and consumer is the vision given by most commercials. They never hint that the Good Life does not necessarily come from accumulating more; it can come from wanting less. The Franciscans realized that although the TV commercial format is often abused, it is neither good nor bad in itself. They decided that if it can promote things of the body it can promote things of the spirit, too.

One telespot shows several preschool children scribbling with crayons on brown paper bags. Their faces are aglow, fresh and innocent. But when they pull the bags over their heads we see they have turned them into masks, fierce and fearsome. Then with quick cuts we see adults wearing masks—the nylon stocking stretched over the gunman's face, the klansman's white hood, the soldier's gas mask. When the children rip off the paper bags their glowing faces once more fill the screen. A voice on the sound track says, "What have we done with God's face?"

This brings to mind the saying that for the first twenty years we have the face that God gave us and after that we begin to wear the one we made for ourselves. This also recalls an observation that if a woman is beautiful at twenty that is good fortune; if she is beautiful at forty that is good maintenance, and if she is beautiful at sixty that is good character. All of this leads to an awareness of how the inner self sooner or later is reflected in the outer self.

In another telespot, a father and his young son walk along a street. The boy imitates the father in everything he does, in the way he tilts his head, walks, snaps his fingers. They approach a movie boxoffice. The father says, "One adult and one child." The boy says, "But, Dad—" The father kicks the boy on the shins and repeats, "One adult and one child." As they approach the lobby the boy persists, "But Dad, you know I turned twelve last week." The father says, "What difference does a few days make?" In admiration the boy answers, "You're smart. You know how to cheat."

This sixty-second morality play, used on some 300 television stations, served as an inspiration for a high-school senior to make his own one-minute film called "Two-Bit Sins." Nothing shown in the film will send the offender to prison, but everything in it cheapens the spirit. I still remember the scene in which a woman shopping in a supermarket picks up a jar, opens it, wipes her finger across the top of the peanut butter, puts it in her mouth, replaces the lid, and puts the jar back on the shelf. The other scenes showed a driver running a stop sign, a boy sneaking an apple off a fruit stand, a girl furtively slipping a paperback inside her coat, and a man taking a newspaper from the sales rack without depositing coins.

Telespots are often used in religious courses to stimulate discussion; a booklet comes with them to encourage that very thing. They can be used to show students how to explore the spirit with a home movie camera, a tape recorder, and some imagination. These statements about the inner life can be put in script form even though the scripts will not be filmed.

One such script tells of how commercialism invades Christmas. It calls for scowling shoppers shoving each other, disgruntled clerks glaring, hands grabbing, price tags galore, red-nosed reindeer, and a dozen other quick shots. On the sound track *Joy to the World* is partly drowned by the clang of cash registers.

Another student wrote a script calling for quick cuts of neon signs, slag heaps, garish storefronts, jukeboxes, beer can litter, and a dozen other daily sights. On the sound track a voice reads the psalm that tells of how beautiful is the world that God has given us.

This juxtaposing a psalm with what is happening on the screen brings to mind a brief film made by the Family Theater in California. On the screen a husband and a wife are shown packing; they are evidently preparing to leave each other. On the sound track the words of Psalm 55 are heard twice, once in a man's voice and once in a woman's:

> If some enemy had insulted me,
>   I could bear it;
> If my foe had risen against me,
>   I could hide from him.
> But it was you, my fellow companion,
>   my comrade, my friend!
> How glad we once were together,
>   walking in procession to the house of God!

Call it a visual poem, if you like. A visual meditation. A visual homily. How long a sermon would it take to make you feel the anguish and the tragedy of separation the way that four-minute film can make you feel it? What is more, it makes you realize how an ancient psalm can fit right into the last half of the twentieth century once an artist gets his hands on it.

I don't promote the use of film, I told the Trappists, out of a belief that the *word* is dead. Even when it was a fad to say that the printed word has had its day, I didn't believe it. The popularity of the printed word was at low ebb ten years ago, but anyone who has observed the ebb and flow of life should have realized that, in time, print would come back into favor. And so it has.

Ten years ago newspaper publishers were beside themselves wondering where they could find young people willing to fill the vacancies in their staffs. The situation was so bad that the *Wall Street Journal* sent hundreds of high school teachers to journalism schools, on well-paid fellowships, hoping that the teachers might interest their students in careers in journalism. In 1974 there were 48,238 college students enrolled as journalism majors, an all-time high and more than three times as many as ten years earlier.

Ten years ago a course in writing was not apt to be filled. Today a course in writing is almost certain to be oversubscribed. Students shunned campus publications ten years ago, but now the staffs of such publications are crowded and new publications are being started.

A dozen years ago a retired professor, a man near eighty, asked of me, "Do students write poetry anymore?" The question was so out-of-date, as though he wondered if they still rode in stagecoaches, that I felt embarrassed about it. I told him that students don't want to be creative now in any way except in making films. I was distressed at the time by the irrational rush to films, even though I had helped pioneer film studies in schools. There were times when I regretted helping films find a place as an academic discipline. Fanaticism is always distressing, especially if it invades an area you care about. Now, however, film is regarded with better balance and if a retired professor asks me today if students are writing poetry, I will say, "Yes, a great deal of it. The bulletin boards are covered with notices of poetry readings. The college literary magazines are filled with verse." So it seems that God and Gutenberg, who were supposed to be dead a decade ago, are alive and well, indicating that the word is not dead, spelled either with a small *w* or a capital *W*.

I promote film, not because the word is waning, but because film, like all art and all technology, is a gift. I fear as much as anyone the fruits of technology when they are used to excess, but I never forget that those fruits are gifts, something like talents. If someone has a talent he had better use it or pay the price of frustration. And so the gift of film had better be used, properly used, or else there will be a price to pay, the price of being out of touch with the times. When teachers begin to feel out of touch, whether in sociology, theology, science, or literature, they start asking for advice on what films to use.

Another reason for using films to explore the soul is that spiritual concerns of the past don't change, but the way of expressing them does. Messages of the past repeated in the manner of the past will bore most people. Scholars prefer the exotic, the esoteric, the dim and hidden path, but the mass audience can only be reached in the current mode. The translations of old truths must always be made at some altitude, the way *The Stray* and *William* translated two teachings of the New Testament into today's terms. Truth ought never be vulgarized in translation. When cheapened it loses much of its truthfulness. How inharmonious to speak of truth in less than a truthful manner.

The best reason of all for using film, I told the Trappists, is that they can say some things to you in a way that books cannot. I hastened to add that books can also say some things in a way films cannot. After preaching this for a quarter of a century, only as recently as last week did I come upon two films that made me realize the truth of it more than ever, perhaps because they touched upon something in my own life. Both were documentaries made by the BBC, one about a war in Burma, the other about a missionary in India.

In Burma during World War II, I was assigned to write a military history telling the story of Vinegar Joe Stilwell, the airlift across the Hump, the Ledo-Burma Road, Merrill's Marauders, the Kachin Rangers, and Wingate's Raiders. Were I to reread my own manuscript today it would not bring back the grimness as completely as that documentary put together from old combat films thirty years after the event.

A few days ago, while watching a documentary about the work of Mother Teresa of Calcutta, I saw starving infants, scarcely more than two large sad eyes, and lepers, twisted and scarred, and I wondered how I could compete in words with such deeply moving communication. The problem was on my mind because my next book is to be about similar subject matter.

The tendency is to say that films show the outward life better than books, and that books reveal the inner life better than films, but that is an oversimplification. Were that true I would not have been talking about films to the Trappists. It all gets down to caring enough about both films and books and being familiar enough with both to know when to use one and when to use the other.

I have said much about the use of films but nothing about their abuse, a subject that could fill a book. Films have a damaged reputation in many places because of their frequent misuse. So often a teacher will show them, especially in a religion course, not because he knows how to use them effectively, but because he is dissatisfied with whatever system he has been using.

To use films in the right way is difficult. I have taught with lectures, the Socratic method, the workshop, and through films, and I find the most difficult system is to teach with films—if it is to be done right. That means films are not used just to fill time but are integrated into the course so that the work of the teacher and the work of the film-makers become one, so much so that it seems to the class that the films were made with that course in mind.

Many people use films without bothering to learn the film-makers way of saying things visually. Even when lecturing to the Trappists I gave a two-hour session on cinematic technique, explaining how a film-maker speaks to them through subjective camera, juxtaposition, recurring motifs, symbols, picture composition, and other forms of visual language. I am so convinced that most people need this kind of instruction that when asked to screen *The Seventh Seal* and discuss it at a retreat house in Massachusetts, I said I would do so on condition that I be allowed to prepare the audience with two hours of instruction in how to look at a film. This does not sound like the kind of thing heard on a spiritual retreat, but it was needed if the retreatants were going to get much spiritual insight from a film as sophisticated as *The Seventh Seal*. So I spoke about the language of film, and *The Seventh Seal* came through the better for it.

The disadvantages of using films are many and painful. There are equipment problems, booking problems, and audience problems. I sometimes feel that if I am reborn I will avoid film with all of its impedimenta and stroll to the classroom carrying only a slim, cool volume of poetry.

The audience problem is the one that puts the teachers to the greatest test. What films to screen and in what order to screen them? Fifteen films might work well if screened in a certain order, but the same fifteen screened in another order might not come off. They need to be screened with a sense of progression and growth. Some films won't be effective if screened early in the course; students need to grow to them and so they are best saved for the end.

One thing is certain, not all films will please everybody. Each semester, at the end of a course, I list the films that I screened in the preceding three months and ask the class to tell me which film they would be most pleased to have made and which ought to be dropped from the course. When I report the results to the class a student may be shocked to learn that a film that thrilled him was boring to the person sitting next to him. People tend to think that what they like, everyone likes. Maybe learning that this isn't true is one of the most important lessons of the course.

A course in religious education, as described here, can be truly educational. It teaches students to look beneath the surface of life, to see the great themes that describe how it is to be human—the themes of love, hate, avarice, arrogance, hubris, death, birth. Relatively few courses in a curriculum make this effort. Most concern themselves with surface squalls that are, in the long view, passing fads. Courses that deal with capitalism, communism, socialism, and democracy, need to be taught, but in the long run the subject matter fades, as did the Twist, hula hoops, and yo-yos. They will join the Roman Empire, the Sung dynasty, and the Third Reich as footnotes, while the great themes go on and on as a part of the human experience.

Great films reveal great themes. They do so by showing the outwardness of things in such a way as to reveal the inwardness of things. The founder of Christianity used this technique. Christ's basic teaching technique was to use definite imagery. He makes us see the sower going out to sow the seed, the father embracing the prodigal son, the Samaritan binding up the wounds. He speaks of such everyday things as the birds of the air, the lilies of the field and the salt of the earth—things that sound like scenes from a Flaherty film. If this technique was used by the founder of Christianity, it ought not be beneath the dignity of a twentieth-century teacher.

The idea of using the outwardness of things to reveal the inwardness of things has been accepted to an extent that films are being used as aids in Sunday School, in high school religion classes, and in college theology courses. Occasionally they are used in Sunday sermons, in spiritual retreats, and in Lenten services. They are used in seminaries, abbeys, and convents, the way books were used for years, to bring spiritual insight. As sources of meditation they supplement, but do not supplant, the observations of Thomas à Kempis, the Epistles of Paul, and the works of Augustine.

This is a good time for films to come into their own in religious education. New ways of doing things slip into the flow of life more easily during times of change. For instance, the belief that a person cannot be both active and contemplative is subsiding. A few years ago the activists would consider the use of film for contemplation as something not *relevant,* their favorite word, for they thought contemplation was a waste of precious time. Contemplatives, at one time, would have considered film too worldly.

Another change is a rebirth of the realization that one can be modern and still have a regard for the past. The *Now* people, not too long ago, considered film their private preserve and anyone who used it as an aid to the spirit would be spoiling it. The traditionalists considered film too brash, and new, and vulgar, and shallow to even touch.

Another change is the realization that an indirect approach to spiritual insights might well supplement the direct approach. Much self-realization must come indirectly. To arrive at an insight through a film, or a play, or a poem, or by letting mathematics or science make us aware of the awesomeness of creation is to find ourselves indirectly. The direct approach, the frontal attack on the spirit through the fierce light of contemplation, has a place, too, but if that is the principal source of self-knowledge it is apt to lead to self-consciousness. To find God and self through the things of everyday life is a more natural way to do so than through the extremes of analysis.

Films are useful in this indirect approach because they lack the definite, clean edge of a moral tract or a catechical answer. They have the blurred edges of life itself. No matter how blurred the edges, though, they cannot rival life in subtlety and crosscurrents because as works of art they are to some extent organized and simplified in a more graspable way than is the simplicity and organization found in the flow of life. They come closer to human experience in the midst of the richness of life than does the codification of much religious instruction.

Another change is a growing awareness of what is meant by community of the spirit. The word community used to stress "togetherness"; people working, singing, talking, dancing together. A community of the spirit comes with the realization of how at rock bottom human beings are alike. This springs from some perception of the human condition.

In the final week of my course "Film as Insight," a student wrote a sixty-second script that brought to focus more than some lengthy moral tracts the realization of community of spirit. The finished film would show two dozen quick close-ups of a cross section of humanity—businessmen, hippies, policemen, nuns, Chinese, Africans, pilots, housewives, children, etc. They are all moving in the same direction. Some hurriedly, some slowly, but they are all going somewhere together. Then suddenly we see where they are going: All are passing through the gates of a cemetery. After these rapidly changing shots the camera comes to focus on a tombstone and holds there quietly for what seems like a long time after all that activity. This makes a statement about the shallowness of categorization. It speaks of the brotherhood of man in a way many more pretentious works do not. It makes the statement in the format of a sixty-second television commercial, a format that people have learned to receive information from, and take advice from, in the past two decades.

At the end of the last lecture I told the Trappists about a nun who put a sign outside of her screening room, a quote from Matthew, chapter 10: "What I tell you in the darkness go speak in the light." They were delighted with the nun's wit and saw new meaning in a sentence that they had read in the choir stalls many times. They said they would probably be using films from time to time. And so they have.

6: A Journal Can Be More than "Dear Diary"

My sister, while putting things in order a few years ago, found a diary I had kept at sixteen and sent it to me. What an unkind thing to do! The first impulse was to destroy it. On second thought I realized that as long as it exists in the world it might be one more thing to help keep some balance in my life.

Through the years I have scribbled in a notebook but not faithfully. That's too bad because it is worth doing for many reasons, one of which is that the act of writing hauls to the surface thoughts you didn't even guess were there and encourages shaping those blurs of notions and hunches into ideas you may be willing to stand behind.

One value of this discipline is summed up in a line that John Adams wrote in his journal: "Pen, ink and paper and a sitting posture are great helps to attention and thinking." Since this is the way the mind works, keeping a journal can help give focus to meditation, contemplation, and mental prayer. Putting words on paper might keep the inward act of worship from declining into a dreary droning in the mind, or a scattered flight of sparrows.

The kind of journal I speak of is more of a journey inward than a diary of dailiness. It concerns itself with the ebb and flow of the spirit more than with the comings and goings of the body. It doesn't wholly ignore such comings and goings, though, because they influence the spirit. What should emerge is a picture of sorts, something of an inscape, with its moral horizons and inner atmosphere, or call it the weather of the soul.

Religious orders have been founded on the belief that mental prayer is the force of the soul and should take precedence over every other occupation. Yet no religious order, so far as I know, asks its members to keep a journal as a spiritual exercise. Individual religious have seen the journal as a form of worship and have found relief in it when plagued with the pressures of Jeremiah, who said that the Word was a burning fire shut up in his bones and he was weary of forebearing and must speak.

In time the jottings in a journal can come to mean more to the writer than printed and bound meditation manuals prepared by professionals. "One of the ways I learned to pray is by writing," said Father Edward J. Farrell in *Surprised by the Spirit*. "I began by copying favorite passages from reading, then thoughts and ideas of others, and finally came to jotting down my own insights and reflections from the prayer and experience of each day."

Writing is usually seen as an activity of the humanist rather than that of the ascetic. Too bad the two are put into opposite camps. A former priest said he was uneasy in the Church because he is a humanist and not an ascetic. He must not have realized that a real humanist has to be something of an ascetic, and the other way around. Humanism is not another word for hedonism and asceticism does not mean masochism. A humanist develops a love of simplicity and feels repelled by the showy, the chaotic, and the vulgar, and the ascetic ought to be doing the same. There is a hint of their relationship in something Katherine Anne Porter said of writers: "But we really do lead almost a monastic life, you know; to follow it you very often have to give up something." Ethel Merman said it in a more brassy way, "When I'm doing a show I take the veil." Both humanism and asceticism must give up something. Both are uplifting until they turn extreme and then, like all extremes, they are demeaning. The priest who saw himself as an uneasy humanist caught in an ascetic's life did not have the imagination to see that he ought to be both.

Not everybody should keep a journal as a spiritual exercise. As a way of worship it is no more recommended for all than is reciting the rosary, or going on pilgrimage, or playing the guitar in church. It is for those who feel the inward push to express themselves in the written word. A spiritual director said he would hesitate to urge some people to keep a journal of the spirit because it might make them too introspective, a tendency they already have. He agrees with Reinhold Niebuhr that the self does not realize itself fully when self-realization is the conscious aim. Anyone too introspective will almost surely turn the journal into an *examen,* with its stress on awareness of faults, instead of using it as something that can lead little by little, over a back road, to some self-realization.

In the search for self the journal may show us what we are becoming by revealing what we are imitating. As the devil says in *Screwtape Letters,* "All mortals tend to turn into the thing they are pretending to be." By middle age we have written the script for ourselves. Our friends have reviewed our show years ago. The problem is to catch ourselves delivering the lines, coming in on cue. Words written over a long time might give us a glimpse of our inner selves, help us catch ourselves in the act.

When Eric Hoffer wanted to know something about himself he started a diary to help in the search. In the introduction to *Working and Thinking on the Waterfront,* Hoffer said,

> I began to suspect that all my thinking life I had probably had only one train of thought, that everything I had written stemmed from a central preoccupation, and that I might go through life and never discover this.
>
> I had to sort things out, talk to somebody. So on June 1, 1958, I

began a diary. Toward the end of March 1959, I realized that my central subject was change.

This adventure in self-discovery can go on to the end of life. As the frontiers for outward adventure close one by one, the possibilities grow for inner adventure. With each added year a man should have more to say about what he has learned of life from having lived it. Bernard Berenson made more perceptive entries in his journal at ninety than he did at sixty. Henri-Frederic Amiel made better entries in 1880 than in 1848.

Father Bernard Basset has also observed that as physical growth declines the possibility for spiritual growth increases: "Study the growth of Augustine in his *Confessions,* of Paul from his first appearance in the *Acts* to the last of his letters, Ignatius from the cave of Manresa to his death in Rome as General of a great spiritual army, Thomas More from being an angry young man in London to the tranquillity of prison in those last heroic months."

In studying journals I have found that the entries tend to become more definite as the writer grows older. The generalities are backed by definite examples. It's a matter of learning how to take the small coin of daily experience and convert it into the more lasting currency of general observation, while growing aware that generalization is unreal unless it rests on experience.

Although the diaries of youth are less perceptive, they are still worth keeping. Even mine at sixteen. It gives a picture I couldn't get in any other way. It's like coming upon a wall that bears the pencil marks showing how tall you were at each birthday, or like finding an old family album. How you have changed! And you hadn't noticed.

A diary helps recall the flaws of the past. The tendency is to glamorize the past, recalling only the sunny hours. Without a written record you tend to see a series of events from the vantage point of *now,* forgetting how it was *then* not knowing what turn each event might take. It discourages claiming prophecy for what is really hindsight.

So much of the best in us is lost if not set down at once, for in the realm of the spirit to withhold something is often to lose it, as Santayana observed. Many insights come in a flash and for the moment bring the thrill of seeing a relationship not seen before. Soon the insight fades and loses its magic. There is a chance of keeping some of it, if it is put into writing at the time. When an insight is passed on from someone else we need to re-express it for ourselves or it does not become a part of us. If we express the insight in our own way we enjoy the growth of assimilation, otherwise we become memorizing filing cabinets.

Some of the things that we know deep down can't be told in the marketplace. Emerson would have sounded silly had he paused to tell the butcher many of his thoughts that morning. Fortunately, he wrote them down.

It sounds contradictory to believe that we change inside and also believe that, "Nothing changes the music of the soul." Everyone is born with a tune in his soul that is especially his. When Thoreau spoke of marching to a different drummer he must have been referring to the music of his soul. The tune is audible at an early age. In a short story a nun says of a kindergarten child, "Charles is stuck with dependability. All of his life he will be that way and it will cause him great inconvenience." Dependability is the theme song she heard in Charles' soul, just as concern for change is the tune Eric Hoffer says he marches to. In both cases a few grace notes or sour notes will be added here and there, but the tune plays on.

Thomas Merton may have had in mind the unchanging music of the soul when he wrote, "Keeping a journal has taught me that there is not so much new in your life as you sometimes think. When you reread your journal you find out that your latest discovery is something you already found out five years ago. Still, it is true that one penetrates deeper and deeper into the same ideas and the same experiences."

It takes a long-range look at life to see such patterns forming. Trying to understand how it is to be human from listening to the daily newscasts is like trying to tell the time by watching the minute hand on a clock, both give fragmentary information. Only when you have lived long enough and remembered well enough or kept a record of your inner self can you begin to see that there is a plan. As Marcia Davenport said in her autobiography, *Too Strong for Fantasy:* "Only from the perspective of age is it possible to see the real design in the network of lives which, interwoven with our own, make us the individuals we are."

A journal may help you find some meaning in your life. As soon as you sense a pattern, you know that all is not chaotic. You need the consolation of finding design, or else you feel that life is absurd. Aware of this need, Father Joseph Powers, S.J., wrote in the January 1972 issue of *Worship:*

> Whatever our experience in our world may be, it must be grounded somehow and integrated within some framework which gives it and us coherence. Without this grounding and framework, our lives become merely a series of unrelated episodes, disconnected points in a random wandering line. We have a religious symbol for this kind of meaningless, groundless, directionless existence: hell. Each fragment of our experience and the total span of it ask the same question over and over, "What does it all mean?"

There is a healing effect in giving form to something, in making things add up, in bringing order out of chaos. It is good for the psyche to arrange a jumble of experience into some inner mosaic.

A student observed that some people pay an analyst fifty dollars an hour to keep their journals for them. He had found that his journal could be a shelter for confidences, a place to make himself freely heard. It helped preserve, amid all of the sound and the fury, some silence within. A nun told me that when life gets hectic and she is too much troubled she writes it all down, knowing that when she rereads these frettings a month or a year from now they are not apt to seem important. Anaïs Nin, disliking to burden others with her fears, said she turns to her diary and "I rest my head here and weep."

A daily piece of writing can serve as a safety valve. Saint Augustine used it to unburden his conscience. No matter how disheveled the day, Emerson said that all of its disasters seem less painful in the evening once they are recorded. After working hard all day as a longshoreman, Eric Hoffer often returns to his apartment in bad temper. "After a glass of hot tea and some fruit, and particularly after writing a few lines, the irritation fades more or less."

Anaïs Nin said that she can't control her daemons but has learned to cage them: Anger, jealousy, envy, revengefulness, and vanity she locks up in her diary. Martin Luther found that to rage against his enemies helped him to pray better. If the spent anger leaves more space in the heart for prayer, that alone is a good reason for writing it all down.

A journal can also alert us to how low our daily intellectual and spiritual incomes really are. Once appalled by such poverty we may do something about it, such as turning to writers, or to individuals, or to experiences capable of enriching. Most daily routines demand physical and nervous energy but ask little of intellect and spirit. The after-hours of fragmented conversations, newspaper stories, and television shows do little for the inner life.

A journal could also make us aware of things left undone. Men are condemned, in Matthew 25, not for anything done, but for six things left undone. This leaving undone is what Irwin Edman, in *Philosopher's Holiday,* called death-in-life when writing about his former students at Columbia:

> There is only one thing by which I continue, with a foolish and persistent naivete, to be surprised. I expect, somehow, that a student ten years after college will still have the brightness and enthusiasm, the disinterested love of ideas, and the impersonal passion for them that some develop during their undergraduate

days. Time and again I have run into them, and wonder what the world has done to them that that passionate detachment should have gone. I know some of the things, brutal or familiar enough to the point of banality: a family, the struggle for a living, a disillusion with the status of contemplation in the nightmare of a violent world. But it is not revolution or disillusion that surprises me; both are intelligible. It is the death-in-life that assails the spirits of young men who had been alive when I knew them in college.

There is a positive side to this, too. A journal can make us aware of the unfolding of our gifts. They don't all bloom at once. Each gift has its season. Growth of spirit will not be hurried. It may be so slow as not to be observed except with a long view. Not to be aware of growth is to miss a chance at serenity, to miss the calm at the core that comes with a sense of harvest.

To enlarge consciousness, or at least not to let it dwindle, is a problem. So much of life is a droning blur, scarcely more than sleepwalking. A sense of the preciousness of experience is a natural gift for some, but most of us need to develop this. I have found that committing experience to writing not only preserves it but shows its importance. Aware of this, Anne Morrow Lindbergh prayed in her early diary (*Bring Me a Unicorn*): "God let me be *conscious* of it! Let me be *conscious* of *what* is happening *while* it is happening. Let me realize it and feel vividly. Let not the consciousness of this event, as happens so often, come to me tardily, so that I half miss the experience. Let me be conscious of it!"

Feeling the same need, another sensitive woman, Virginia Woolf, wrote in her diary: "I mark Henry James' sentence: Observe perpetually. Observe the outcome of age. Observe greed. Observe my own despondency. By this means it becomes servicable. Or so I hope."

By expressing a desire for awareness, each of these women, at least for a while, was more aware of the moment. Each had to renew the effort later, no doubt, because it is not one that can be made as a perpetual vow. To live in the instant, to realize the *here* and the *now,* is an achievement, rare and fragile and elusive. This alertness to the specialness of the instant, that it is the only one like it you will ever have, brings some understanding of what is meant by "the sacrament of the present," the only fragment of time you can really use.

You might dull awareness as a protective coating, in self-defense, because you are on the receiving end of so much communication: the musak in the elevator, the jukebox in the snack shop, the transistor radio in the park. The omnipresent TV set. Auto horns, billboards, magazines, newspapers— receive, receive, receive. So pull in the antennae, glaze the eyes, and turn off the hearing aid. You teach yourself not to attend and this lesson carries over to things that deserve attention.

You may be more willing to receive if aware that, sooner or later, a blank page in your journal will stare back at you. Maybe you will even become a good listener. If you know how to listen, you will get credit for being a great conversationalist and will never lack entries for your journal.

Just as you need a plan for prayer you will need one for keeping a journal. Spiritual directors and professional writers give identical advice for going about doing what they must do because both are talking about the same thing, communication. The advice is identical because whether you are trying to speak to God or to man you are stuck with your own human psychology. I came to realize this when reading an article that the religion editor of United Press International wrote on how to pray. To gather advice he read books on the subject and interviewed spiritual directors.

The first piece of advice that spiritual directors gave was "Pray each day at the same time." Professional writers tell a beginner to set aside a definite time for writing each day and keep the rest of life from intruding on it.

Have an habitual place for prayer, was another suggestion. It is more difficult to bring the mind into focus when on the run or in an unfamiliar place. Many writers find they work best when they sit down to the same typewriter in the same room day after day.

Posture in prayer is something considered by spiritual directors. An uncomfortable position may be a distraction, but a too comfortable one discourages concentration. Reclining in an easy chair may cause the mind to sag as much as the spinal column, because the mind and spirit tend to follow the example set by the body. Writers find they get down to work faster if they sit up to a desk or table.

Prepare for prayer with a brief period of devotional reading, is another suggestion. The UPI religion editor wrote, "This helps you to make the transition from the hectic world of daily routine to the quiet mood of prayer. It enables you to focus your attention on God, which is both the precondition and the purpose of prayer." Writers, too, suggest a period of preparation. They find it helpful if they edit or rewrite something they had worked on the day before. Most find that certain writers make them feel like writing, and so they spend a few minutes reading the work of a kindred soul to get the courage to face the glare of a blank piece of paper.

Long-windedness is not a virtue in prayer. A spiritual director told the religion editor that it is better to pray briefly and regularly than to indulge in marathon prayers one day and then skip several days. It is also better to write a couple of pages every day than to churn out a stack of pages once in a blue moon.

Be specific in prayer, is another piece of advice spiritual advisors gave the editor. Nearly every book written about prayer stresses definiteness. "It is better to thank God for a particular blessing, to ask forgiveness for a particular sin, or to ask a particular kind of help for a specific individual than to indulge in sweeping and usually meaningless generalities."

The book *The Elements of Style* by Strunk and White has this to say about being specific: "If those who have studied the art of writing are in accord on any one point, it is on this: the surest way to arouse and hold the attention of the reader is by being specific, definite and concrete. The greatest writers— Homer, Dante, Shakespeare—are effective largely because they deal in particulars and report the details that matter."

Spiritual advisers agree that you ought to pray whether you feel like it or not. The UPI article says, "It is your will, not your fleeting emotions, which you offer to God in prayer. Even the greatest saints go through frequent 'dry periods' when they do not feel the least bit pious, but they keep on praying." Professional writers also agree that it is not safe to sit and wait for inspiration. They believe that a writer should write whether he feels like it or not, that inspiration comes from sitting down and writing, not from waiting.

The close parallel between praying and writing is a good argument for combining the two efforts in a journal. The parallel suggests that the activities of humanists and ascetics are not complete strangers. It makes clearer what Katherine Anne Porter meant when she said that a writer's life is almost monastic and that to follow it you very often have to give up something, and what Ethel Merman meant about taking the veil.

It is a loss to all of us that more housewives, doctors, religious, all kinds of people, fail to set down on a day-by-day basis their vision of life. Such a journal if honestly kept would bring consolation to everyone because it would reveal that in the most ordinary of lives we are not alone: others have tramped this same terrain, suffered stretches of aridity and spiritual chills, and rejoiced at the rare oasis.

What to do with all of those journals? Religious might leave theirs to the archives of their community; laymen to a local historical society or to the archives of a university or to children, grandchildren, or great grandchildren—the more distant the generation the greater the interest. All observations become of interest in time. During the centenary of the Civil War the diaries of humble soldiers were published, but no publisher would have been interested in those observations the day they were written.

Even if no one ever reads your journal, it's still worth keeping. Virginia Woolf wrote in hers, "The truth is that writing is the profound pleasure and being read the superficial." Marianne Moore wrote in her journal that writing should not be done for fame and fortune but mainly as a felicity and as a way of intellectual self-preservation. To write for the sake of felicity, and intellectual self-preservation—and as a way of worship—that is more than enough.

7: All Ritual Inherits the Aches of Communication

When I heard that Duke Ellington was dead, in the summer of 1974, my memory turned back to Christmas night of 1965. That night, as he said later, he was able to do in public what he had been doing in private for years. He took a twentieth-century idiom, jazz, and used it to translate the advice of the ancient psalmist: "Praise God in his sanctuary: praise him with the sound of the trumpet; praise him with the timbrel and dance; praise him with stringed instruments, and upon the loud cymbals and the high-sounding cymbals. Let everything that has breath praise the Lord."

In all of these ways Duke Ellington and his orchestra praised the Lord with a concert of sacred music in the sanctuary of the Fifth Avenue Presbyterian Church. In front of the golden oak pews with their burgundy seat pads, in front of the stained glass windows, they praised the Lord. The whole setting spoke of tradition, conservativeness, affluence. The printed program said that even the Presbyterian Church with its starched classical image is reaching outward. How far outward was indicated in the list of patrons: the Five Spot, the Half Note, the Newport Jazz Festival, and Father Norman O'Connor.

Duke Ellington explained: "In this program you will hear a wide variety of statements without words, and I think that you should know that if it is a phrase with six tones it symbolizes the six syllables in the first four words of the Bible, 'In the beginning God,' which is our theme, we say it many times, many ways."

Ellington played a piano solo, *New World A'Coming*. He explained it as the anticipation of a very distant place on land, at sea, or in the sky where there will be no war, no greed, no nonbelievers and no categorization. Where love is unconditional and no pronoun is good enough for God.

There was honest communication when Cat Anderson praised the Lord in the way he can praise him best, with a trumpet that goes high, higher, highest. On a bass viol, John Lamb did what the psalmist said, "Praise Him with stringed instruments." Nobody took the psalmist more at his word than did Louis Bellson, who in six minutes of percussion solo praised Him upon "the loud cymbals." Lena Horne sang and Brock Peters sang and Bunny Briggs tapped, *David Danced before the Lord with All His Might*.

Ellington wrote in the program:

> Communication itself is what baffles the multitude. It is both so difficult and so simple. Of all men's fears I think that men are most afraid of being what they are—in direct communion with the world at large. They fear reprisals, the most personal of which is they won't be understood. How can anyone expect to be understood unless he presents his thoughts with complete honesty? This situation is unfair because it asks too much of the world. In effect we say, "I don't dare show you what I am because I don't trust you for a minute, but please love me anyway because I need you to. And, of course, if you don't love me anyway, you're a dirty dog, just as I suspected, so I was right in the first place." Yet every time God's children have thrown away fear in pursuit of honesty—trying to communicate themselves, understood or not—miracles have happened.

I left the concert more aware of how varied sacred music can be, and now, more than ten years later, still remember that Christmas night with pleasure. This is strange coming from someone whose personal taste is best reflected in the worship at Westminster Abbey.

The Abbey is still a reverential place even though two million tourists pass through it each year. Religious services are held several times daily with strict vergers making sure that all is calm during that time. As a leaflet explains, "The Abbey was built above all that God might be worshipped in the beauty of holiness and in the holiness of beauty."

I especially like to sit in the choir stalls for Sunday matins. Often the first line of the opening hymn is, "Lord of beauty, thine the splendour." How appropriate when sung in a splendid spot saturated with prayer for nearly nine hundred years. To sit there surrounded by music and stone that declare the dignity of man, that proclaim his possibilities, is something that moves powerfully on the soul. It makes me proud to be a human being.

During one of the noonday sermons in Westminster Abbey, a priest recalled that as a boy confined to a dark room with the measles he had played gramophone records all day. He listened again and again to a certain passage. It said something to him. For the first time he realized that music is a language. This led him, in time, to understand how architecture says things, too, and to see color, light, shadows, and other inanimate objects used in ritual as forms of communication.

When he began to see ritual as communication he approached it in a new way. He realized that ritual needs to change somewhat with time and place, and with groups and individuals. He understood then that, while a form of worship may be legislated, to expect it to have meaning to everybody attending is as futile as requiring everyone at a party to have a good time.

Different times encourage different ways of worship. The tempo, mood, tone, values, and concerns of the times influence the approach to the Almighty. The emotional outpourings of the medieval mystics would give most of us the creeps in the second half of the twentieth century. The ritual of princely pomp, traditional for centuries, lost its effectiveness in civil life, and eventually in the church, after the passing of the aristocracies.

Of course, there are exceptions to this, as to everything. Princely ritual can still be effective if the setting and the occasion are right. The setting of Westminster Abbey allows for the pomp that would be out of place in suburbia, where a guitar mass is more fitting than it would be in the Abbey. As for the occasion, Edith Wharton spoke of traditional ritual as giving "a sublime frame" to the three great events of human life— birth, marriage, death. Rather than discard the sublime frame, perhaps we should reserve it—Latin, incense, vestments, all of it, for sublime occasions: weddings, funerals, Easter, Christmas.

Yes, even Latin should be used on sublime occasions. Auden wanted Latin prayers to remain in Latin, saying, "Rite is the link between the dead and the unborn, and needs a timeless language, which in practice means a dead language." Perhaps the Mass, too, should be reserved for the sublime occasions, because any form of communication that becomes routine is apt to become perfunctory.

For centuries the statement was made, and was true, that no matter where you go in the world you will find the Mass the same. That ritual needs to vary from place to place is a recent realization. A generation ago most of us would have been startled to hear that before long a mariachi band would play at the eleven o'clock Mass in the Cathedral at Cuernavaca, Mexico. As soon as ritual was seen as communication, the mariachi band naturally found its way into church as a Mexican idiom.

The Council Fathers at Vatican II showed an interest in developing a ritual in harmony with the local culture. In Article 37 of the Degree on the Liturgy they said, "Even in the liturgy, the Church has no wish to impose a rigid uniformity in matters which do not involve the faith or the good of the whole community. Rather she respects and fosters the spiritual adornments and gifts of the various races and peoples. Sometimes, in fact, she admits such things into the liturgy itself, as long as they harmonize with its true and authentic spirit.''

This led to experimentation in the liturgy. Anyone who went into such experimentation with his eyes open couldn't help but feel fearful. Once he realized the variety and complexity of all the audiences he wanted to reach, he must have felt like running back to traditional forms of worship and slamming the door behind him. Audiences differ by ethnic origin, culture, age, education, sophistication, personality, and a thousand other more subtle ways. At the risk of discouraging experimentation, let's look at some of these audiences.

The most dramatic experiments, and on the whole the easiest to bring off, are those done with ethnic groups. In India, for example, the general principle used in experimental liturgy since 1970 is that bodily attitudes should conform to those habitual with Indians: sitting on the haunches, standing without shoes, and replacing genuflections with the profound bow of the Far East. In the penitential rite, priests and faithful sometimes perform the *panchanga pranam:* the prostration in which five bodily members touch the ground—the hands, feet, and head. Vestments conform to a simplified Indian style; oil lamps replace candles; the use of incense increases. At the beginning of Mass the celebrant is sometimes welcomed by the *arati,* a shower of flowers.

In Japan an Irish priest says Mass in harmony with the Japanese style of dining: on a *tatami* matting, he sits back on his heels in front of a table only a few inches high. The experiment was introduced to an old people's home attached to Our Lady's Hospital, in Tokyo. The elderly ladies were delighted with the new liturgy, adapted to Japanese etiquette; the constant changes from kneeling to standing to sitting during Mass had been hard on their old bones and muscles, and was confusing to new converts.

Even with the best of good will in these matters some things can go haywire. Some parishioners in India asked that no Indian traditions be reflected in their liturgy. "We want to get away from all of that." Some Japanese, eager to copy the ways of the West, rejected an architect's drawing of a church with an oriental motif. Some Irish missionaries when told to be alert to ethnic preferences became so alert to their own ethnic roots that they forgot it was the parishioners' preferences they were looking for, and so they built a church in the shape of a shamrock in Africa.

Even within the same ethnic group the cultural difference can be great. Monsignor Knox, a convert to Catholicism, was always aware that in England what separated contemporary Anglicans from Roman Catholics was not so much theology as taste. What Protestants disliked most about Catholicism had nothing to do with dogma but with legalism, plaster statues, mumbled Masses, and Mediterranean piety.

In rewriting the *Manual of Prayers,* Monsignor Knox said:

> Among the barriers which divide us from our fellow countrymen and make it difficult for them to understand us is one which has a certain, though limited importance, and has always forced itself on my attention. In our vernacular devotions we do not use the same idiom as Christians outside the Church. And this is the more serious in that prayers used by the Church of England are, by general admission, models of dignity and faultless prose rhythm. No convert, I think, has ever failed to experience a sense of loss over this difference.

Even within the same culture the mature and the immature are no more apt to find meaning in the same ceremony than they are in the same book. The age of the audience is a major consideration in every form of communication.

The Children's Mass in my time meant that at the ten

o'clock service all the children sat together in the front pews, but the liturgy was no different from that at the other Masses. Now, at a Moppett's Mass in Florida parables are told through puppets. At a similar Mass in Indiana, university students help with a liturgy that inclues a clown, a dog, a rabbit, and a turtle. On Christmas morning, in our town, a priest dressed as Saint Nicholas for the Children's Mass, dramatizing the fact that a bishop is the ancestor of every Santa Claus who comes bearing gifts. A few hours earlier, at Midnight Mass, an organ, a trumpet, and a dozen ballerinas announced joy to the world and helped the people hear the herald angels sing.

Many adults would have been uneasy at the Saint Nicholas Mass and most small children would have fidgeted through the midnight service. Sermons that feature clowns, puppets, and turtles might be wonderful at four but they don't do much at forty. Everyone must grow up whether he wants to or not and as he grows he changes in spirit as much as in body, maybe even more. As he grows he needs to change in his way of worship as much as in shoe size.

Would that the problem were as simple as merely trying to reach children or adults. The level of sophistication among children is varied enough, but among adults the variation is confounding. For example, a series of sermons based on Adrian van Kaam's book *Religion and Personality* might be wonderful in a university chapel but all wrong in most parishes.

Personality differences are the hardest of all to deal with. To oversimplify, there are in the main five audiences, reading from left to right according to personal tendencies—radical, liberal, middle-of-the-road, conservative, and reactionary. I was amused to hear an English priest say that when he was young he divided saints into three political parties—Labor, Liberal, and Conservative. These bands of coloration are usually used to describe the political spectrum, but they are also found in religion, art, education—everywhere. In music the preferences range from champagne melodies to acid rock; in poetry, from the disciplined sonnet to the fragmentations of the *avant-garde,* and in motion pictures from Disney to underground films. Newspapers, books, and magazines also reflect this wide range of preferences.

In worship, too, the bands of coloration are bound to appear. To try to reconcile all of these groups into approaching God in the same way is a thankless effort doomed to disappointment. It is easier to get a middle-of-the-road Catholic and a middle-of-the-road Jew to sit down and reason together than to reconcile either of them to the extremes of right or left within his own religion. When free to move in a free society people tend to band together by spiritual coloration more than by religion, education, or neighborhood, but these latter do have a bearing on spiritual coloration. Birds of a feather *do* flock together. We are drawn to those who, as the Quakers say, speak to our condition.

If a priest is going to hold a Mass that might be called "Pizza and Beer/Jesus is Here," he ought not urge everybody to come. If he intends to stand on his head at the Canon just to show he is ecumenically in touch with yoga, he should be sure of his audience before he tries it. And if he is starting a litany to Saint Jude the Patron of Lost Causes, he had better be sure of his audience before he makes an announcement in the bulletin, or else he might be left holding one more lost cause.

Some people need the sense of poetry, of mystery, and some want a religion as complete as a scientific report. Many need a bookkeeping type of religion because they take a bookkeeper's approach to all of life. They need lists of venial and mortal sins, nine-day litanies, five decades to a rosary, an exact number of days of indulgences. This gives them something to hang on to but would drive an artist up the Gothic arch.

This spectrum of coloration was further complicated in recent years by the entrance of "the third man." The expression, "the third man" was coined by a French Jesuit, writing in a French journal in 1967, to describe a growing number of Christians. He said the first man is the conservative Catholic who wants to keep the Church as it was. The second man is a progressive Catholic who wants to renew the Church. The third man loves the Church, enjoys her traditions, and yet chooses to stand apart from the great body of canon law, at least for the moment. He selects his doctrines and would not consider arguing with a pope or a bishop about them. The sacraments are wonderful, if they can help him, but if they don't he doesn't feel guilty about it. He says, in effect, "Law is great, and I am not a rebel. But if canon law doesn't really fit my life, then I make decisions independent of it."

All of these individual differences cause the Church more frustrations than they cause us as individuals. We can take the attitude, you go your way and I'll go mine, when we come upon someone of a different spiritual coloration. That may be a breach of charity, but we have been through that before. The Church, though, is stuck with everybody. She teaches that every soul is worth saving, even those of reactionaries and radicals. Imagine being stuck with all the fanatics who turn whatever they touch into a caricature. The price of charity can be steep.

Finally, consider the needs of the "group people" and the "loners." These contrasting personalities are found in the spiritual life as surely as in social life. In worship, group people prefer celebration that is outgoing and action-filled, and loners prefer quiet and contemplation.

Groups create a prevailing wind and loners are buffeted by it. There is always a prevailing wind in religion as there is in art, politics, and other human affairs. Right after World War II, as an example, the missal at Mass was so much a part of the prevailing wind that anyone who didn't use one was made to feel like a second-class citizen. After Vatican II, however, the missal joined the catechism as another book that publishers lose money on. These books were replaced when religion was caught up in the spirit of revolt that energized all of life from 1965 to 1970. In those years anyone who was not an activist was made to feel lacking, just as he had been made to feel an outcast when he did not fit neatly into the old-fashioned religion. It is always the group people who say with intensity how the wind should blow.

The plight of the loners is without solution because they cannot organize to promote their cause. If they could they wouldn't be loners. In our time if you can't organize you haven't a chance.

The loner, feeling that he must have a little time "to belong to himself," as the French say, drifts more and more away from the group. Not at ease with being a part of mass emotion, he keeps searching for silence at the core. He knows that solitude is not a void to be feared but something to be filled, a form of creative effort that makes demands on his inner resources each day. Could it be he has an intensity of religious feeling without much devotional feeling? Liturgy requires devotional feeling. Some loners, needing a gentler, softer music of the inner life, have turned to the East, even baptizing some of its religion into Christian yoga.

The loner needs celebration, all right; everyone does. It is the concept of celebration that makes him uneasy. For most people celebration must be evident to the eye and to the ear; they feel the need to give praise in public. The loner is at his best giving praise in private. He feels guilty in the presence of those who celebrate with more outward vigor. At times, he even wishes he could be like them, but try as he might he still finds that processions and communal singing make him uneasy.

He is able to celebrate life by moving slowly through it. A walk in the woods brings more of a religious experience, makes him more aware of God's presence in the world, than a ritual enlivened by candles and incense. He prefers a God-made cathedral to a man-made one, sensing that not only churches are sacred but that the whole earth is. His intuitions tell him that calling the church holy and the hearth profane narrows God down to a small piece of property.

The group people have split into two camps, those who want a swinging liturgy and those who prefer a frozen liturgy. They are so at odds that they have started publications promoting their causes. Although they disagree, they understand each other better than they understand the loner.

The danger is that the loner and the group people will take whatever form of worship comes most natural and say that this is the way everybody must perform. Not to be hostile, that is the problem on both sides. To be content with repetition and still forgive those who search, or to search and not belittle those who feel at ease with repetition—that's an ideal easier to write about than to bring off.

Group people sometimes resent the loner's withdrawal. This resentment was reflected in a complaint that a young retreat master made about silence. He said that on a retreat it is often difficult to get some people to talk during meals because they have the old-fashioned idea that silence during a retreat is a good thing.

The people he complains of have just come in from a world where noise is a health problem, where there is small chance of putting together two thoughts without having them fragmented. They come from a place infected by urgency, where green spaces have been capped by blacktop and the charms of nature are arched over with freeways all a-blur with people more interested in getting around than in going some place.

The young retreat master should understand that if people feel lonely and adrift it is not for a lack of hearing enough words on a given day. Their problem is that they have not had a chance to put all of that stimuli into patterns. The more the senses are bombarded by stimuli, the more the silence of meditation is needed, and the harder it is to come by.

Anyone capable of contemplation ought to be encouraged, even helped. Yet to require contemplation of everyone is like requiring everyone to run a hundred yards in ten seconds. Some people just cannot bring it off.

Balance is what group people and loners need. David Wilkerson was aware of this when he wrote *The Cross and the Switchblade,* a book describing his work with voluntary helpers in the New York slums: "Each morning these young men and women would rise, have breakfast and then spend the morning in prayer and study; it would be an essential part of their work. I have long discovered that too much running around without a base of quiet meditation produces little of value."

Dag Hammarskjöld reached that conclusion, too. He was a modern man who allowed the active and the contemplative to meet in him to a high degree. During the day he was buffeted about in international diplomacy, but at night he wrote in a journal reflections of deep spiritual concern.

The Church, if it really believes that all souls are worth saving, must be kind to both group people and loners, even when they find it difficult being kind to each other. The Church and the group people and the loners all need to face the inconvenient fact that aloneness for most people is destructive, but for some too much togetherness is equally destructive.

This may sound as though I am making the matter of differences far too complex, but really I am oversimplifying. The appalling complexities are far beyond my ability to describe. To develop these differences just a step more: for some people the Almighty is a light burden and for others a heavy load. Some think of Him as personal and as knowable as a neighbor, while others are aware of their infinite ignorance of God. Some are so in awe of God, overwhelmed by creation and mystery, that they are resigned to everything, but there are those who must argue and, like Job, demand to know *why.* All of these people can't be expected to pray in the same way. The danger is that the more articulate will take the attitude, "We know something about God that you don't know," and try to make their way the approved way.

Another difference shows up in the matter of searching. Some people are more in need of the search than others. This even shows in the walk of life chosen: some want jobs that can be learned once and for all and repeated over and over; others prefer a continual challenge free of routine. When it comes to worship these tendencies will out, and indicate a need for both a set liturgy handed down and approved by an organization and also a fluid, more personal way of worship.

Then there is the problem that some people will use ritual as therapy. No doubt the creating of something can do good things for the psyche. Maybe this is one legitimate use for ritual; certainly it is a humane use. But what about those who do not want to be a part of other people's group therapy? How many hours of their lives should they be willing to dedicate to that? It is a delicate question involving charity.

There is a fine line between worship and idolatry. There is always the danger of liturgy for its own sake instead of for God's sake. Ritual for its own sake is vanity. Ritual for the sake of the participants reflects a thoughtfulness, a concern for others that is charity. For the sake of God, it is love. It is easy to perform ritual for its own sake. It is more difficult to perform it for the sake of the participants. To perform it for the sake of God takes the greatness of a saint.

By now it should be clear that through the ritual of his preference each person gives himself away. All communication is self-revealing. For example, the less sophisticated the person the more he feels safe repeating the same rite over and over in exactly the same way. The repetitious rite at its best lifts the heart and settles dreads; at its worst it is an aberration. The sophisticated person is interested in releasing his emotions in more subtle ways, and so he turns to the arts. Sophisticated ritual at its best is man at his best, and at its worst it is man revealing his affectations.

That ritual should fit the time and the place and the person is not only necessary for good communication, it may also have a moral dimension. Isn't it a breach of personality to have a man take part in a rite for which he has no feeling? To force a man into a ritual that is not for him is a form of cruelty. Such force won't be physical in our time, but it may be moral. Physical or moral, such force treats man as less than man. If there is one thing that should be done with an open heart and embraced with both arms it is the way one communicates a reverence for the Almighty.

Required attendance at ritual presents a problem in communication. Among professional communicators, for example, a theater manager might be pleased to have a law of required attendance because that would be profitable, but the artists—the writers and performers—would feel uneasy in the presence of a captive audience, an audience that will be present in body but not in spirit.

Asking a person to attend a certain church because he lives at a certain address is another failure to see ritual as communication. No one buys a certain book, or reads a certain magazine, or watches a certain television program because he lives on a certain piece of property. In all forms of commercial communication, men seek the things that touch them at their level of development. In religious matters a man might find his needs better filled in a church three parishes away, and yet he is expected to go to a certain church because he lives on a certain piece of property. The commercial communicator would feel frustrated if he had to make his appeal along parish lines; what he aims at are audience levels. The commercial communicator knows, because dollars and cents have taught him so, that, in the main, some people prefer an intellectual approach to things and some an emotional approach, and a blessed few prefer some balance.

All of this awareness of complexity of audiences should either cause the Church to throw up its hands in despair or do

what professionals do, settle down to a serious study of communication. How much of a sense of communication is a gift
and how much can be developed, no one knows exactly. Certainly quite a bit of the skill can be taught; if not I have wasted
much of my life trying to teach it.

Until now it has been assumed that any ordained minister
has the ability to make ritual come alive. Every minister is not
a Renaissance man with something for everybody, so perhaps
some should lead ritual and some should not. The best conceived ritual, like the best conceived play, may suffer through
performance. Even God must get bored with some liturgy. A
tremendous desire to get through to an audience and a fear of
being boring are necessary attitudes for anyone trying to communicate something. Those who think that they are looking
good no matter what they do are almost sure to be boring, and
those who think that whatever they say is of interest to everybody will be dreary communicators.

The dreariness will be reflected mainly in their "timing."
They will put too many words in a sentence, stretch an anecdote too long, include too many insignificant details, string
together too many glittering generalities. I have just come
from a commencement at which the speaker held forth for
thirty-two minutes. The same speech given as a lecture in an
auditorium, or during a class period, would not have been too
bad, but in the context of commencement, a ritual of many
parts, the speaker lost the audience by talking about fifteen
minutes too long. The day before, a Baccalaureate Mass lasted
an hour and a half, at least fifteen or twenty minutes too long.

Recently I went to a church I had never been to before. A
likeable young priest gave a first-rate sermon. Then instead of
stopping he went ahead and gave another first-rate sermon. So
he ended with a soggy effect. I felt pained because here was a
man with zest in his language and sense in his observation, yet
he lacked a sense of timing. But I was wrong. At the end of
Mass he said, "I didn't realize I spoke so long. I apologize. It

won't happen again.'' He is going to be all right because he knows when his timing is off and it bothers him. He realizes that everything he does isn't interesting just because he does it. That is the kind of humility a communicator needs.

Moses showed an awareness of timing when he sang to the Israelites: ''May my instruction soak in like the rain. . . . '' Every communicator needs the timing that lets what he has to say soak in like the rain. Too slow is ineffective and deadly; too fast is like a downpour on parched earth, so much runs off without a chance to soak in.

Better too short than too long, because when something goes too long it tends to spoil whatever went before it. The multiple ending is the biggest timing flaw in commencement addresses, banquet speeches, and sermons. Time and again the speaker gives promise of ending but then takes off again; he keeps buzzing the field while the audience awaits with hope each effort to land.

The Archbishop of Dublin must have a good sense of timing. He was concerned enough about it that in May of 1974 he decided to permit laymen to distribute Communion in some Dublin churches, observing that distribution of the Eucharist to a large congregation is so time-consuming that the priest tends to rush all of the liturgy.

In Dublin the Church has built a Communications Center to give the clergy a chance to learn to work through newspapers, magazines, radio, television and motion pictures. The communication document issued by Vatican II planted the seed from which the Center grew ten years ago. The document recommended that in each country a national office of communications be started. An Irish Archbishop, Thomas Morris, of Cashel, worked on the document in Rome, so when he returned home it was natural that he appoint someone to look into the problem.

The organizer of the Center, Father Joseph Dunn, said that his program has no fixed goals. ''We don't expect that everyone who takes a course will use it directly in the mass media. Up until now the clergy had no opportunity to study media and so media did not enter into their calculations. For another thing, the direct approach to preaching has not been too helpful in the past. Let a man learn broadcasting and then apply to preaching what he has learned in broadcasting. As professional producers we give a priest a cold assessment of his work, something he rarely gets.''

Father Dermot Carthy, after taking a short course at the Center, talked about a few things that came through to him. He spoke with awe of a professional broadcaster who became known to the students as ''the coroner'' because of his post mortems in which he would pick out the ''priestly'' word or look or approach. ''By the end of the week you could pick them out yourself—if you were still using them'' said Father Carthy.

''All in our group found themselves being dissatisfied with everything they wrote. Some words didn't seem just right, sentences were too long, the introduction was dull, the thoughts expressed didn't hang together as they should, and everyone had a sentence or two that conveyed nothing. All of this was with our prepared scripts, which we were not supposed to use in televised performances. The playback revealed even more frequent lapses when we spoke without our text. A few hopefuls used their manuscripts when on camera but that candid eye caught their furtive glances. If a speaker was not well-prepared, the half-done spadework showed up quickly.

''We learned by doing that a radio talk is often easier than a television talk because you read your script. But hesitation, or dullness of voice, or poor diction are much more harmful on radio than on television. If someone being interviewed ''umms' and 'aahs' on radio it is painful, but on the television screen his groping for words could be effective. And words that look good to the eye when written can sound wrong to the ear when spoken.

"In preaching—they used to tell us in the seminary—strike oil in five minutes or stop boring. On television they allow you fifteen seconds. So you must cut out every vague, unhelpful word. The importance of a good opening strikes home quickly when you see examples of both gripping and dull introductions being produced in the studio as you watch."

The director of the Communications Center, Father Dunn, thinks maybe the greatest thing that happens in his studios is that religious come to realize how much time and trouble professionals put into their work. It helps them understand that good intentions are not enough; technique is needed too. They learn what Jacques Maritain meant when he said that piety is no substitute for technique.

For years I admired the effective way clergymen used radio and television on the BBC. Only recently I learned that the church has had its own training school for fourteen years, the Television and Radio Training Centre, at Bushey, on the outskirts of London.

A member of the staff, the Rev. Leslie Timmins, said, "Parsons and social workers all have the same problems, they find it difficult to cope with mass communication. They use jargon like anyone else; they make pious noises instead of saying something effective. Religion is about communication, and people have to learn the new tools of mass communication."

Oh yes, there is a danger of getting "showmen" as directors of ritual. Quintilian, the Roman teacher, said something worth remembering: "I hold that no one can be true orator unless he is also a good man." Goodness is a factor in the effectiveness of anyone leading ritual, but goodness alone will not bring it off.

Even before it gave much attention to communication, the Church was blessed with individuals who had a natural gift for reaching others. By their very way of being, perhaps it was their deep goodness, they showed a sense of anthropology.

One such individual, an anonymous Franciscan, was described by Bernard Berenson in an entry in his diary dated May 31, 1948, at a villa near Florence:

> For a week my parish church has been turned into a brilliantly lit drawing room, where the villagers were attracted to come and listen to the eloquence of a Franciscan who harangued them about their duties as Catholics, as men, as Italians. He addressed them in languages of their own brew without inhibitions, and from the age of three upward they listened and had their ears filled with the rhetoric they love. Then yesterday a procession with bands, gorgeous garments, flowers, gaiety of every orderly kind, to my private chapel. All in all a work of entertainment going straight to the senses and heart of the villagers (or rather suburbanites), that Communists and similar performers cannot rival. Think of the dreary harangue in Gorky's *Foma Gordeev* whom his fellow picknickers, revolutionists like him, had to stop! No, anthropologically the Church has all the innings. (*Sunset and Twilight,* p. 82)

That sermon, so effective in Italy in 1948 would not be too effective in the United States in the 1970s. It might be less effective in Italy today, too, because the more a culture becomes saturated with the mass media, the less effective becomes the sermon as a format.

To develop new formats of worship is work for the artist, for communication at its best is art. To develop a ritual that is genuine for a certain time and place takes all the talents that great artists have been blessed with. Ritual and art are related, because no matter if one wants to communicate with God or with man he works from the same basis of psychology.

The church used great artists for its ritualistic settings: they built the cathedrals and added paintings to the walls and composed the music, and in so doing contributed glorious chapters to the history of the church and to the history of art. But the greatest artists were not invited to lend their talents to the heart of ritual. It would indeed be wonderful if universities today could offer a course called the Literature of the Mass that would include the names of Dante and Chaucer and other great writers through the centuries on up to the present.

If an artist were to write a liturgy of the Mass, he would want to know what is the unchanging core, what is the heart of the matter. For the answer he might well look at a film, *The Eucharistic Prayer of Hippolytus,* produced by the Murphy Center of Liturgical Research at the University of Notre Dame. It is an unusual film because of its directness, simplicity, and clarity, characteristics we expect to find in great teaching, but which come as gifts in scholarly work.

As the film begins, a narrator in modern dress walks into a third-century Roman home and says that it is predawn on a Sunday in about the year 210 A.D. As he speaks, Romans in the garb of those days enter in the background. They arrive as singles and in pairs so as not to call too much attention to themselves. They move with a quiet dignity that is almost choreography as they place their gifts on the table.

The chief elder enters, the deacons secure the doors, and the liturgy of the Eucharist begins. The Christians exchange greetings of peace in awareness of Christ's admonition that before the offering everyone needs to be reconciled with his brothers. The deacons select as much bread and wine as will be needed for the service. Other gifts of the faithful are set aside to be distributed to the poor.

The chief elder and assembly pray in Greek. Contrary to popular opinion the language most used at the time was Greek, not Latin. The Greek population of Rome was larger than the Latin population. The old Latin families were still pagan at the start of the third century, and so the Roman churches were attended mainly by Syriac and Greek-speaking people.

The service lasts seventeen minutes, indicating that the early Christians had better "timing" than their successors. Perhaps their fear of the Roman soldiers improved their timing, and if that is the case, we would do well to throw a few liturgists to the lions just to improve their sensitivity.

The remaining forty minutes of the film is given over to a

panel discussion about Christian worship. One of the panelists, Father Leonel L. Mitchell, explains why the prayer of Hippolytus is of interest to the whole Christian church. "This prayer, in English translation, was used a decade ago by the National Student Christian Federation for a celebration of the Eucharist. It was used as a means of getting behind some of the controversies of the fifteenth, sixteenth, and seventeenth centuries that divided Christians on this whole issue of the Eucharist. If we are trying to do what Our Lord Jesus did, and to do this 'in memory of Me,' as He said, then it is helpful for us to go back to see just what is involved in 'doing this.' I think that this original laying out of the liturgy helps us recognize that in the Eucharist we do four things: we take bread and wine, we bless them, we break bread, and we distribute them to be eaten and drunk by the faithful, just as Jesus did at the Last Supper. And we have here in this service, this Eucharistic prayer, and in the directions that precede and follow it, just an outline of a basic service without any of the decorations that have been added over the years.

"Some of our problem is that today we don't like Victorian houses and all the Victorian gingerbread that we've stuck onto our liturgy. People want to strip it off and say, 'This is ridiculous. It doesn't belong there.' But getting back to this gives us a chance to see the actual weight-bearing walls of this liturgical house, and to see what the framework is. So that when we strip off all the later decor and all the additions, we can see what the real framework is. And then begin to say, 'All right, if we're going to put modern decorations on it, at least we'll make sure we have the same house when we are finished.'"

The reason for having an artist build on the old foundations of liturgy is the same as having an artist build on the old foundation of a house. The true artist, whether he admits it or not, has such a reverence for life that he cannot clutter it up with inadequacies. His willingness to sacrifice himself to get it "right" is a religious attitude. Anyone who lifts life is praising

God the Creator of Life. If art is really communication at its best, an artist is a man of charity, because he brings light into the world.

An artist would find it especially inharmonious, especially depressing, when something is badly done in God's name: shabby ritual, a disheveled parochial school, a sloppy church supper. A Renaissance hermit, Paul Giustiniani, was careful to set his table properly for a frugal dinner. In his determination not to become a slob in his aloneness he turned a simple meal into a form of liturgy. He encouraged other hermits to be exact in such matters, for he knew that the spirit tends to follow the body and that once the body goes sloppy a sagging spirit can't be far behind.

This sounds as though I see manners as an aspect of worship, a form of communication, and so I do. Call it civility if you will, or charity, or love, or *agape*. John Tracy Ellis said he has always believed that courtesy and good manners are qualities not unrelated to good morals. Manners are a part of humility and it is humility that makes men bearable to one another. The things Saint Paul recommends would make an outline for a book of etiquette: "Always patient and kind/ never jealous/ never boastful or conceited/ never rude or selfish/ not taking offense/ not resentful/ no pleasure in other's sins/ delights in the truth/ always ready to excuse/ to trust to hope/ to endure whatever comes."

All of this has to do with lifting life. As I said before, if God is the author of life, then whatever lifts life is good and whatever lowers it is evil.

Thomas Merton had enough of the artist in him to be pained by how in the name of the good and the true somebody makes things ugly. This awareness of what might be called the immorality of something badly done is revealed in *The Sign of Jonas:*

> Dylan Thomas's integrity as a poet makes me very ashamed of the verse I have been writing. We who say we love God; why are

we not as anxious to be perfect in our art as we pretend we want to be in our service to God? If we do not try to be perfect in what we write perhaps it is because we are not writing for God after all. In any case, it is depressing that those who serve God and love him sometimes write so badly, when those who do not believe in him take pains to write well. I am not talking about grammar and syntax, but about having something to say and saying it in sentences that are not half-dead. Saint Paul and Saint Ignatius Martyr did not bother about grammar but they certainly knew how to write.

Imperfection is the penalty of rushing into print. And people who rush into print too often do so not because they really have anything to say, but because they think it is important for something by them to be in print. The fact that your subject may be very important in itself does not necessarily mean that what *you* have written about it is important. A bad book about the love of God remains a bad book, even though it is about the love of God. There are many who think that because they have written about God they have written good books. Then men pick up these books and say: "If the ones who say they believe in God cannot find anything better than this to say about it, their religion cannot be worth much."

Two liturgical scholars, Father James D. Shaughnessy and William Storey, agree that in time people worship the way they want to worship. Father Shaughnessy said, "The periphery moves the center. Liturgy isn't something developed by the hierarchy or the inner circle. All they do is approve of something that has been well-established out in the boondocks."

Professor Storey enlarges on this, "I think the hierarchy lives out of the people's faith. People worship the way they want to worship. They worship out of the way they apprehend the Gospel. They pray and sing and so form extemporaneous prayer. Sometimes they even write it down. That becomes liturgy. But these days we have a special problem—we have highly organized churches. We have highly organized liturgical commissions, and we have popes and bishops and synods. All think they can make liturgy. I don't think they really can make liturgy, not in the long run. I think they can help the people form the kind of liturgy they need and desire. What we really need is a great sensitivity to actual needs, a sensitivity to what is going on, and a regard for our tradition. The tradition is usually found in the universities. Through historical theological studies we discover what was the center of our faith in the past. We can discover through our own experience what is the center of our faith in the present. Then we, all of us, can try to bring that together. We hope that we will get the blessing of the Pope, bishops, and all kinds of people."

When asked if the amplified guitar and the Eucharistic prayer of Hippolytus can be wedded without too much difficulty, Professor Storey said, "No problem there at all, provided the amplified guitar is played properly. And provided the Eucharistic prayer is proclaimed properly. It's a question of artistic skills here more than anything else. Any prayer can be ruined, either by a lack of faith or by a lack of diction."

This liturgy for the people by the people is also hemmed in by dangers. The main danger is that it will become entangled in the cult of the amateur, a cult that was thriving in the late 1960s, but is less lively today. *Amateur* is really not the right word for those who disdain professionalism, those who think sloppiness is wonderful, who act as though there is virtue in doing something not very well. Inept people may be virtuous, but there is no virtue in ineptness.

Some people seem to feel that in a lack of style there is salvation, that the vulgar life is holy. They seek the artless, common, and mediocre and suppress anything with distinction. Maybe they have a false idea of what simplicity is. In any aspect of life there is no substitute for simplicity, the ultimate in style. In daily living, as in art, to cut free of the curlicues, to let the essentials show through, that is the secret. In worship, too, the motto might well be: not too much rigmarole.

Perhaps the worst thing would be a ritual written by a committee. Think of all those compromises! A prayer written in committee is not apt to have much inspiration in it. Statues of individuals who have passed on inspiration are plentiful in the park, but how many statues are there to committees?

The to-do over ritual has died down in the mid-70s, or so it seems to me. The problem arose because for years ritual was a fixed matrix into which generations were poured, an exercise in repetition rather than in a changing creative effort. Since ritual was not allowed to unfold in easy stages of evolution, it suddenly went through the throes of revolution, with the result of too-hurried innovations. To plough under traditional ritual so fast is dangerous. Too many familiar landmarks disappearing too fast causes a loss of orientation that brings on confusion. Trying to communicate with someone who lacks orientation is like trying to speak to him in a language he does not understand.

The lines were drawn between those who wanted to keep the traditional and those who wanted to throw it out. The immovable objects met the irresistible forces. As usual, the promoters of new ways claimed they were throwing out the authoritarians of the past only to be revealed as equally authoritarian. Instead of saying let's have both the old and the new, and finding it exciting, the tendency was to turn it into a case of either/or, a case of us against them.

Surely it must be evident to both sides that a homily that uses slides of *Peanuts* cartoons could have meaning for the young but might make older people feel uncomfortable, just as guitars and bongo drums at Mass make them uncomfortable. If older people prefer the organ, the rosary, the silent meditation, why not let them have those things?

The trouble is that everyone tends to look upon any suggested form of worship in light of how well it fits *everybody*. Speak to a pastor about the journal as a form of worship and immediately he sees himself trying to convince *all* of his parishioners to start writing down their meditations. He is appalled at the thought, and should be. He should be just as appalled at expecting everybody in his parish to make a novena.

Professionals in mass communication are burdened with a dark realization that the Church might as well face up to: nothing reaches everybody in every audience every time. Sooner or later all of us feel the numbing touch of accidie, the noonday devil, because sloth, boredom, and downness are part of being human. The liturgy will never be devised that does not sometimes pall. The lifeless performance comes into all of life. We are wrong to believe that we can *always* do what we can sometimes do. The only consoling thought is that accidie is a rogue familiar to everyone who has given serious thought to the life of the spirit.

During this time of transition, being aware that there is no panacea but still searching for variety in worship, how far should we go? It is a matter of prudence and of a common sense that is really uncommon. We are searching for harmony and balance, the hardest thing in life to come by, as the Greeks said two thousand years ago. Even the search is a form of worship. The answer will never be completely found any more than God will be completely found. Searching in the realm of the spirit is not like searching for a lost cuff link, a case where something is lost one minute and then, presto, we have it completely the next minute. In matters of the spirit there is always the search and the adventure, the shadowy corners and the anxious moments.

Surely it is not asking too much that all worship be done at some altitude. If the Japanese tea ceremony, or marachi bands, or tribal drums are used in worship they should be used in a way that lifts life. It would be ironic to lower life in praise of the author of life.

Ronald Knox said that stained glass at its worst and sorry statuary and sugary hymns ought to be discouraged, but never forget that these are only accessories of religion. Ceremony is not religion. If one says, "Yahweh" and puts "for thine is the kingdom and the power and the glory" at the end of the Lord's Prayer, and avoids the Latin language, these are secondary matters of communication, but they are not religion.

Religion is a deep awareness of God as the basis of all things. It is a response to reality apprehended as divine. When God is seen everywhere, that is two-way communication and maybe the highest form of worship.

Worth remembering is a teaching of Zen Buddhism: If you want to hold something in life, hold it gently as you hold water in the hand. Love, wealth, health, hold gently. Friendship and life itself hold gently. If you care about the arts and the sciences, hold them gently. Ritual, too, hold gently like water in the hand. When you grasp you don't have anything.

8: Education Can Prepare the Spirit for Worship

A thoughtful young man said that he used to be interested in a politician's views on specific issues, but now he is more interested in the man's character. As he spoke, the thought struck me that to some extent a similar shift of interest has come about in religion. People used to be more interested in the formal teachings of the Church, in what a politician would call "the issues." They debated dogma and argued their ideas in books and magazine articles.

Theology is no longer such a struggle of ideas. Theology is trying more and more to be a channel of communication that helps direct the search for fulfillment. This grows from a feeling that the fulfilled person is a living, breathing *Te Deum,* a form of worship. And so the growing interest is in what religion does: Does it bring peace of soul? Does it sensitize the spirit? Does it help a human being in becoming what he is capable of becoming? Does it organize daily living? Valéry said that Christendom is tending toward a faith that is the intuition of order: "the relatively modest dogma that God is not crazy."

"The theological problem today," Karl Rahner said, "is to find the art of drawing religion out of man, not pumping it into him. The redemption has happened. The Holy Spirit is in men. The art is to help men become what they are."

The truth of Rahner's statement came home to me because of something I learned while teaching design. Each year I have come to realize more and more that my job is not to pump design ability into a student but to search out what is already there and to help him uncover it and bring it to the surface. It is a matter of helping him become what he is capable of becoming. In a quarter of a century, I have not found a student without some sense of order deep down inside himself.

The Church used to pump in the kind of information that can be stored in a computer and retrieved at the press of a button. Rote education produced the kind of mind that is most at ease with rote worship. This stress on filing answers distracted ministers from the art of drawing to the surface the best that is there and refining the spirit in the process. It is simpler to ask that something be memorized than to try to sensitize the sensibilities. Filing information is easier on the teacher because all it requires is that he be a dutiful taskmaster, but when he tries to sensitize the spirit, the stress is on the quality of the teacher as a person.

Not every spirit is sensitive enough to handle religion, or patriotism, without tragic results. Northern Ireland comes to mind. There Protestant and Catholic are causing people everywhere to observe: See these Christians how they hate one another. A good many spirits in Northern Ireland are not ready for either patriotism or religion. History is full of such dark tales of people whose spirits were unprepared for strong inspiration. Hitler and Stalin were not ready for patriotism and so they swung to the extreme of nationalism. Savonarola and Peter the Hermit were not ready for religion and so they went on to become fanatics. Fanaticism results when warped spirits try to handle strong feelings. A sense of balance and harmony has not been developed.

The Church with its lists of answers felt sure of itself, elated almost to the point of euphoria, and saw little need to promote the spiritual search. In the past decade, though, stress has been on the search. This seems more in touch with the way a human personality grows, or at least ought to grow.

The stress on searching is not new. Even the apostles said, "Lord, teach us to pray." Early in the Christian era, Saint Augustine said that if you want to know whether a man is a good man don't ask what he believes or what he hopes but what he loves. What he loves reflects the quality of his inner life, the result of his searching, or of his failure to search.

Education has not been teaching the kind of love that lifts life. We love so many wrong things that although our diploma count is high, we don't show signs of being an educated people. We don't reflect the attitudes that one has a right to expect to find in the educated. The attitudes that we would like to see are such that both secular and religious educators might well join hands to develop them.

Secular and religious teachers should not have trouble agreeing on these four characteristics of an educated man:

He vibrates in the presence of quality.

He keeps growing in spirit.

He works out his destiny with a sense of dedication.

He develops a poetic vision that keeps expanding.

The educated man vibrates in the presence of quality whether he finds it in a person or in a poem. He senses the difference between quality and luxury. He prefers the first-rate to the third-rate in architecture, television programs, books, paintings, newspapers, and in any other thing he comes across in life. He is high minded. He has aims, standards, and ideals.

We are uneducated diploma-bearers because we too often prefer the shoddy to the substantial. We find that "junk pays." Just check television and radio popularity ratings, book sales, boxoffice statistics. Which sold the more copies, *Valley of the Dolls* or *The Collected Poems of Robert Frost?*

As Leo Rosten wrote: "When the public is free to choose among various products, it chooses again and again the frivolous against the serious, escape against reality, the lurid as against the tragic, the trivial as against the serious, fiction as against fact, the diverting as against the significant.''

The cluttered Las Vegas approach to every town reveals no love of quality. The cities, despite the graffiti, are terribly gray and sad. The shattering decibels of traffic, acid rock, and machinery have created a noise level that has become a health problem. All of this commotion does not spring from a zestful love of life, but from fidgets, twitches, and lack of discernment. All of these jaded concerns reflect spirits that can scarcely be called educated or religious. All of this was accumulated by people who are worldly, but do not love the world, do not cherish and revere God's gift.

This insensitivity to quality brings to mind the invocation written as far back as 1931 by the Council for Preservation of Rural England: ''From all destroyers of natural beauty in this parish and everywhere; from all polluters of earth, air and water; from all makers of visible abominations; from jerry-builders, disfiguring advertisers, road hogs and spreaders of litter; from the villainies of the rapacious and the incompetence of the stupid; from the carelessness of individuals and the somnolence of local authorities; from all foul smells, noises and sights—good Lord, deliver us!''

An old-fashioned word, *collected,* used by horsemen and spiritual directors, is no longer heard but ought to be. When a horse is collected he has a unified way of going, he is not all spread out, and when a soul is collected it has unity at the core and is not splashed all over the landscape. The thing of quality is collected. It reflects such restraint that it is, at once, ascetic and aesthetic. In these days all of the sound and the fury make it difficult for horses or souls to be collected.

A love of quality can be developed through a love of art. Religious education did not show much interest in art until recent years, and secular education has not done as much for art as it should. In speaking of unfortunate gaps in his education, George Kennan, the retired ambassador, said, "No one, to the day of my graduation, had ever taught me to look understandingly at a painting, or a tree, or the facade of a building." Although nearly half a century has passed since the day of Kennan's graduation, most of the students who receive their doctoral degrees this year will not have been taught to look understandingly at a painting, or a tree, or the facade of a building. No matter what the student majors in he should be led to love the best that man has made, because it changes the quality of his inner life and that, in turn, changes the quality of outer life. If all of our diploma bearers really loved quality, our landscape would not be so ugly.

Art has a special place in religious education and in worship because it is concerned with the importance of things, the intrinsic worth of everything that God chooses to hold in existence. A way to define an artist is to say he has the touch that makes everything he creates seem important, even a nonrepresentational shape. Van Gogh makes us see a simple chair in a new way; Rembrandt helps one realize the importance of a beggar. Such films as *La Strada, On the Waterfront,* and *The Set Up* are examples of how the artist shows the importance of people, even those who are less than admirable. In the day-by-day brush with the literal we tend to think that the only important people are those we would like to entertain at dinner. Artists like Fellini, Breugel, and Tolstoi have a way of showing importance even in the ordinary.

Since the Church is interested in developing wisdom, that is reason enough for it to concern itself with the arts. Wisdom grows with its roots in a culture, one that is a flowering of abstract thought and of an awareness of concrete realities in the here and now. Wisdom and vision can't exist in a half man, the thinking man; the feeling man must be there, too.

Today religion shows signs of admitting that art can communicate to the human consciousness certain subtleties of truth not knowable in any other way. It senses that there is a danger of giving so much stress to the intellect that the intuitions are lost for lack of use, or lost out of mistrust, or lost because one feels guilty about them. Perhaps religion was more interested in the thinking man than in the feeling man because the intellect seems safer than the intuitions and the emotions. One can sin with the intellect as well as with the emotions, but intellectual sins are cold ones and the cold sins, until recently, caused less concern in our culture than the warm ones.

In recent years, many young people revolted against the cult of the rational, shunning structured dogmas and memorized admonitions and ritual pieties. They swung from Apollo, the god of the highly organized, to Bacchus, the god of the free-wheeling, and in so doing zoomed right past that balanced middle ground where wisdom dwells. They turned to the arts, but no one had taught them how to handle such strong stuff, and so they began to break form wherever they found it and to use the word ''art'' to cover a multitude of horrors. In giving themselves over to their feelings they got out of touch with reality as much as did the rationalists on the other extreme of the spectrum. They became characters in a Chagall painting, floating above the earth, dreaming their Eastern dream of mysticism as their parents had dreamed their Western dream of materialism, all expecting a utopia. None of this sprung from a love of quality but from a frustration that turned to ideology for a solution. None of it reflected favorably on education, either secular or religious.

The growth of the spirit right up to the end of life is another natural concern for both secular and religious education. While doing research on a book, *Why Americans Retire Abroad,* I became painfully aware of how many spirits stop growing. To find out why some 300 thousand elderly Americans have pulled up roots and tried to transplant them in foreign soil, I went to Italy, Greece, England, Ireland, Portugal, and Spain for interviews. During many hours of conversations with the elderly I learned that our approach to retirement has been lop-sided. We stressed the material to the exclusion of the spiritual.

Whenever someone writes on the subject of getting ready for retirement, ninety-nine times out of a hundred he means getting ready financially. The impression gets around that if a retiree has no money problems, he really has no problems. During my interviews I found that impoverishment of mind and spirit is a more usual problem than impoverishment of the purse.

A friend of mine, a priest, sees this impoverishment as a religious problem, and he is doing something about it. He has rented rooms in a large old house to establish the Forever Learning Institute. It is not the usual Senior Citizens Center where old people come together to play bingo and cards and exchange information about the latest aches and pains. The Forever Learning Institute is for people fifty-five or over who want to keep growing in mind and spirit. Retired university professors offer classes in art, languages, history, film, literature. A lecture series draws from specialists in the community: journalists, tax authorities, librarians, and medics.

Everyone who comes to the institute must have the courage to change, for growth means change in the right direction. They realize that, like it or not, change will continue. As the author-anthropologist Loren Eiseley said, "There are things down there still coming ashore. Never make the mistake of thinking life is now adjusted for eternity."

The tendency is for people to come to a screeching halt in growth of the spirit. Sometimes this happens before the body stops growing. It can even happen in the teens. Some get into the twenties and even into the thirties before the tragedy occurs. The fortunate ones keep the spirit growing right up to the end. When someone stops growing in mind and spirit, he is dead from the skin in. He breathes a little every day, and so is not legally dead. No one can bury him without getting into difficulty with the law, and while the law may declare him not dead, it cannot without stretching a point declare him alive.

When someone stops growing, his likes and his dislikes freeze. At fifty he likes the same books he liked at twenty, the same films, the same television shows. As for the interior furnishings of mind and spirit, he never puts. anything aside and never adds anything new.

When someone stops growing in spirit he begins to fight change. I have seen that happen in some students. After paying thousands of dollars in tuition it seems they ought to want to be offered a hand that will help them lurch up onto the road and point them in the general direction of an education. Instead, they cuddle up to their adolescent attitudes and want to be the same cozy selves on the day of graduation that they were on the day of freshman orientation.

Anyone who stops growing in mind and spirit goes through the rest of life with blinkers on his eyes and stoppers in his ears. He never really sees anything or hears anything. His opinions are a set of rubber-stamp clichés that he keeps filed away inside a narrow mind. Whenever something new turns up, be it a painting or a play, a political program or an insight into theology, he reaches inside for one of the clichés and rubber-stamps the object, and withdraws to the cell of his complacency.

If you want to witness this attitude at its most dramatic, travel abroad and watch the tourists. Several million of them get up enough nerve each year to leave home in body, but too many lack the courage to leave in spirit. Jets help them change the landscape all around them, but the landscape of their minds never alters. They are annoyed with anything unfamiliar, be it a brand of coffee, the plumbing, or cultural patterns. They want the whole universe paved just like the street they live on.

They walk through castles and museums and cathedrals and are bored. If they were as aware of their sagging spirits as they are of their aching feet, it would be a hopeful sign. The sense of awe is dried up in them and they seldom show wonder, unless you want to count the many times a day they say, "I wonder how far away the bus is parked."

Many of these people come from well-furnished homes, but the furnishings of their minds and spirits are inadequate. Their houses may be expensive, but they are hemmed in by small imagination and caged by fears of their own making. They have lost their freedom.

I use the word *freedom* with caution because so many people seem to think it means *complete* freedom, as though there is such a thing in this life. At best we exchange one set of restrictions for another. Freedom is finding a saddle that fits fairly well. Even the best fit chafes sometimes, but it needn't cause an open sore.

This matter of freedom brings up the point of how the educated man and the religious man ought to work out their destiny through dedication. Without a sense of vocation they are not apt to feel free. Anyone with a sense of vocation does in life what he feels needs be done. He works for the love of the task and the satisfaction that comes with it. He doesn't do something simply because there is money in it. If he does he is living life on money's terms and not on his own. If he is overly security-conscious he will never live larger than life, perhaps he won't even be able to live life-size. The drive for security tames life too much, makes life wan, lacking in zest, devoid of style.

If he finds a way of life that brings satisfaction and is also encrusted with money that is wonderful. Then he can say with joy in his heart: all this and money, too!

So far I have put this on secular terms, the kind someone teaching in a tax-supported school would be allowed to discuss in the classroom. He can point to the economic advantages of doing things well: It's good business. A priest said to me that Dale Carnegie's book *How to Win Friends and Influence*

People is all about charity but that Carnegie, instead of stressing this primary reason for being kind to others, stresses a secondary aim: financial gain.

Yet the problem of finding a vocation is most worth considering on religious terms. Martin Buber brought it into sharp focus when he said that while we begin with the task of discovering ourselves, our pre-eminent concern is not with our own salvation but with finding a way to "let God into the world." In working with a sense of vocation, daily life is hallowed and God is let into the world.

For years the Church used the word *vocation* to mean religious vocation, but now it admits a larger meaning. Our vocation is our inner inclinations. It is what we can do—repair gadgets, cook, teach—anything we have a special feeling for. Everybody is a man of destiny. No matter how humble the job it can be a destiny. I knew a waiter, a laundress, and a blacksmith who turned their humble jobs into vocations, into destinies, by the very way they approached them. They worked out of love of the task and the thing done with love is somehow greater than itself. The integrity of their work was a form of adoration. Their nobility of purpose so lifted life it was an act of worship, a way of letting God into the world.

Religious educators need to work harder at communicating the idea that the *way* something is done is at the very foundation of religious life. No activity is religious if it lowers life, and none is secular once it lifts life. *How* a thing is done is rock-bottom communication that goes beyond all words and turns an act into one of worship or into a blasphemy.

The form of communication known as intuition is worth considering in any discussion about vocation. Religious education must be concerned with intuition if it sees it as a channel for communicating God's will. Since God isn't limited to working through the intellect only, maybe sometimes he nudges the intuitions.

Living in harmony with these inner promptings is what the

Greeks called happiness. These nudges, spoken of in every age, are described by Aristotle, Goethe, Yeats, and Klee. Plato spoke of a *daimon,* saying that God gave one to every man as a connection between the human and the divine. Christian writers speak of the promptings of the Holy Spirit and of Divine Grace. Socrates referred to "a kind of inner voice" which he first noticed as a child. Although he was a philosopher accustomed to using his reason, when the court asked him to decide whether he preferred death or exile, he knew the decision was too important to leave to his head. He returned to court saying he had chosen to die, feeling that if his decision were wrong his "internal oracle" would oppose him, but it didn't.

Socrates' description, "a kind of inner voice," might lead people to expect to hear words, perhaps even listen for complete sentences. While spoken words or written words might trigger the inner response, still the intuitions deal in inclinations, pushes, nudges, and hunches, all unfortunate descriptions, I admit, but they are better than "voices" because they refer to silent communication and so more accurately describe the experience.

Renoir said that life went best for him when he allowed himself to move with the nudges, "like a cork on a stream." When he ignored his intuitions, things went wrong. Ronald Knox used a similar metaphor, "Keep your hand lying light on the tiller, ready to catch any breath of guidance that God will send you."

This awesome awareness of God's will won't come in a voice from a burning bush and it probably won't arrive full blown, either. It will need to be worked out creatively. We are back again to the idea of searching. Saint Paul was aware of the need for such searching when he said, "Try to discover what the Lord wants of you."

A documentary film, *Dancing Prophet,* produced by the Franciscan Communication Center, helps us realize that a vocation is not something imposed, but something awakened. We are not only created by a divine force but also have a creative force within us that helps in the creating of self. We are told that the Kingdom of God is within and the redemptive force is there, too. We are to find this force and reconcile ourselves to the direction it urges us.

Some people lack the courage to seek the silence that will allow the promptings to be heard. Of course the silence is hard to come by with all of the to-do of modern life, a kind of spiritual smog that hides the sun. It is easy to be a practicing atheist with all that clutter coming between God and man.

The tendency in a scientific age is to see God at work only in rationality. We are apt to ignore the gaps between rationality, those vast, vague areas of intuition, where some of our best inclinations dwell. We fear that if we follow these inclinations we might be fooling ourselves. No doubt the intuitions can be abused. Rollo May, who writes about all of this at some length in *Love and Will,* admits that such inner guidance requires a fundamental humility. He warns that our convictions are always blurred somewhat by blindness and self-distortion and that the ultimate conceit is to believe ourselves free of illusion. The Greek admonition "Know thyself" means knowing and freely admitting that we are so very human that we tend to see things through a glass darkly.

May says, "The moral problem is the relentless endeavor to find one's own convictions and at the same time to admit that there will always be in them an element of self-aggrandizement and distortion. Here is where Socrates' principle of humility is essential, for psychotherapist and for moral citizen."

This is a problem of delicate balance. Humility might be pushed so far that it becomes false humility. The intuitions might be ignored because they lack the clean-cut edge of logic and the apparent sureness of scientific proof. Each time the intuitions are ignored they grow weaker. Finally we are left holding arid rationalism. A grim, gray fate awaits everybody who thinks that life can be lived out of the head only.

In ignoring inner inclinations we are apt to do whatever we do for shallow reasons. I have known college students to major in a certain area because that's what their friends majored in. It was the thing to do, a fad. There are fads in graduate studies as much as in skirt lengths. At one time the rush was into science, because of Sputnik. Later the rush was to engineering; then into teaching, and now, in the 1970s, law is the in thing but is rapidly giving way to business administration.

Most young people find it hard to accept the mystery of the future. They want to know exactly what they will be doing five years from today. And so they try to work it all out in their heads instead of being sensitive to those inner pushes. They are made uneasy by a sense of destiny. They are frightened to think that destiny is worked out in every present moment and that it is a continual search. It is frightening for them to believe that the present moment is tied to the past and will influence the future. They can't bear all that pressure on the present.

They need the religious sensitivity that Ronald Knox had to the present moment. He did his best to see in the present situation, the present task and in the interruption of that task the working of a Providence. Knox did not always succeed in repressing the sigh, the slight gesture of impatience, the querulous remark, but that is only to say he was not perfect.

It is easier to think of life as blind chance, a spin of the roulette wheel, for that relieves us of all responsibility. It's easier, but less satisfying. Anyone who sees life as a blind spin of the wheel is sooner or later going to find it absurd and slide from there into despondency.

The secular educator can sell the idea of seeking a vocation as a way to happiness. He can say with sureness that a sense of purpose can give a great lift to the heart, and that a lack of direction might be life's heaviest burden. He might quote José Ortega y Gasset: ''And every living creature is happy when he fulfills his destiny, that is, when he realizes himself, when he is being that which in truth he is. For this reason, Schlegel, inverting the relationship between pleasure and destiny, said, 'We have a genius for what we like.' Genius, man's superlative gift for doing something, always carries a look of supreme pleasure.''

The religion teacher can go beyond that. He can tell someone in search of a vocation that whether he is scientist, artist, or laborer he ought to do what he does for the reason Dylan Thomas gave for writing poetry, ''for the glory of God and I'd be a damn fool if I didn't!''

Both religious and secular educators might quote Father Adrian van Kaam, a professor of psychology, describing the glory of man who develops a radiant center of personal thought and feeling:

> He is a person urged on by the awareness of an irreplaceable vocation, a personal mission, a unique presence. Of course, this does not necessarily mean that he does common things in peculiar or eccentric ways. It means that he does things in personal ways, with a personal love, a personal feeling of responsibility, a personal commitment, and in a personal style. He is not a dead element in the community of men, but a personal participant in the mission of society.

I said earlier that an educated man ought to have a poetic sense that keeps expanding all through life. Here again secular and religious educators might join hands. Both will agree that a poetic sense, an imagination of high order, is a spiritual quality that is found in a mature spirit. Rather than try to define this poetic sense I will give examples of it:

E. B. White begins an essay by telling about the time he watched a young girl practicing bareback riding at the winter quarters of a circus. In the center of the ring stood her mother, once a famous rider. White said that the girl was at the height of her physical powers—lithe, graceful, lean. Her mother was no longer lithe and lean.

White says of the girl: She was still young enough to think that as she made one circle of the ring nothing changed.

But, of course, as she made one circle of the ring everything in the universe changed. And she was just a little closer to being the fat lady in the middle of the ring.

Everyone there knew the fact of the event: a young girl is practicing bareback riding and her mother is in the center of the ring. White got more, and he passed it along to us, because he is endowed with poetic vision.

The film *Nanook of the North* is about the life of an Eskimo. It does more than teach us how he fishes and builds igloos. It helps us see how noble man can be when he makes an intelligent use of whatever resources he has. It does that, not through preaching, but through revealing the attitude of the film-maker, Robert Flaherty. It reveals his poetic vision. Many films about Eskimos do no more than tell how they fish or build igloos because the man who made them saw no more than that.

The British documentary *Night Mail* is about the train that carries mail from London to Glasgow. But it is not just about men riding in a mail car futilely sorting letters into pigeonholes. The men who made it had poetic vision. They help us realize that these men are sorting hopes and fears, and that is not a futile occupation. And on down the track we sense people waiting for the postman's knock, for no man can stand to feel forgotten.

If a man has a diploma filed in the attic but lacks poetic vision, we cannot rightly blame him for it. Education makes precious little attempt to develop such vision in him. It may even have stamped out whatever he had to begin with. Education is hard on the spirit for more reasons than I know, but I'll discuss some that I have noticed.

For one thing education is grade-oriented. I am not against grades, mind you, but I am against an excessive awareness of them. If we put too much faith in them, we tend to teach only things that can be graded. It is difficult to grade whether or not a student vibrates in the presence of quality. So we have him memorize twenty-five rules for something or other; that we can grade.

I teach a course in motion picture criticism that stresses film aesthetics. It is nearly impossible to grade. Time and again such courses turn into film history because history is more easy to grade. I have long been tempted to make the change.

The same things can happen in art and in literature. What starts out as a course in art aesthetics might turn into art history for the sake of assigning a grade. A course that had something to do with a love of good writing might become literary history for the sake of the final exam. Courses that started out nourishing a poetic sense turn into a collection of information, when they should be bringing realizations about what God has made, the burden of all art. Information is something we know from the eyebrows up and can be graded. Realization, something known in the deep crevices of the soul, is difficult to pin down.

Another way that education has been hard on the spirit, especially hard on poetic vision, has been through fragmentation. Each piece of information was wrenched out of orbit and sent wandering through the mind, an erratic satellite, lonely and unrelated. Nothing adds up.

Knowing is not important unless it leads to *being somebody*. Memorized information lying inert in the mind is not worth the burden; it needs to nourish a new and admirable way of seeing. Integrating schools isn't good enough; experiences within those schools need to be integrated, too. We have to fragment to teach, that's true, but the very moment we fragment we should assume the responsibility of putting things back together again. We need to show enough of the relationship between things to give some hint of wholeness.

In a review of *The Way of Chuang Tzu*, edited by Thomas Merton, the New York *Times* observed: "There is much in common between Chuang Tzu and Teilhard de Chardin's vision of the universe as an organized whole." To this could have been added Federico Fellini, Sean O'Casey, and Albert Einstein. What a memorable week it would be if students read some of Chuang Tzu, Teilhard's *The Future of Man,* and watched Fellini's *La Strada,* searching for a sense of unity. They should be made aware of a perceptive line in O'Casey's play, *Young Cassidy:* "There is as much mystery in the dirt and the dung as there is in the heavens," and they should consider something Einstein said, "The most beautiful and profound emotion we can experience is the sensation of the mystical. It is the sower of all true science. He to whom this emotion is a stranger, who can no longer stand rapt in awe, is as good as dead."

To see the plural in the singular and the singular in the plural is an aim worth calling educational. If a student catches a fleeting glimpse of unity, it could shape his life. Once the insight sears the soul, nothing is the same.

I have named theologian, philosopher, artist, and scientist in this concern for developing poetic vision. Yes, the scientist—especially the scientist—in his focus on provable truth is a part of the spiritual search. His is an adventure of the human spirit. He can help a student *see* in a way that brings an aesthetic thrill. Anything seen without feeling has not really been seen.

I am aware of what a wonderful thing it is to have an aesthetic experience bring warmth to scientific knowledge, because a university professor, Dr. Roman Visniac, helped me see things in a new way. He believed that in teaching information about nature the teacher ought to help the student feel the beauty of nature, too. He made motion pictures to reveal the beauty. Textbook, charts, and slides alone are not enough for teaching biology, he found, for they cannot tell the whole story. The exuberance and the movement of nature are an important part of the story, a part that can be realized only through film. He really believed that to look into a microscope or through a telescope unaware of a transcendental power is missing much of the glory.

I remember a close-up of reflections on water that resemble beautifully designed abstract paintings in motion. It may have brought me my first awareness of how much an abstract painter imitates nature. Dr. Visniac observed that although the motif of the reflections is repeated over and over in a similar way, no two are ever identical even after millions of years of recurrence, for nature knows infinite variety. In that one observation he was saying something about science, design, and the glory of creation.

Dr. Visniac in showing bacteria under high magnification helped us realize that even the germs that kill us are glorious. The digestive tract of a worm, unattractive when spoken about, is beautiful when enlarged on a screen. The digestive tract, in design and color and nobility of rhythmic movement, is something to stand in awe of. The interior of the heart of a fish embryo is filled with tremendous activity; when enlarged to fill a screen fifteen by twenty feet it is startling in its design, color, and vitality. And the architecture inside plants surpasses the architecture of Gothic cathedrals. And what movement! Had we not been told we were watching a tiny piece of plant enlarged 2,000 times, we would have thought it some ebb and flow deep in the ocean.

Dr. Visniac was a poet, no doubt about it. He wanted to give knowledge about things and also of things. The mind tells *about;* the emotions tell *of,* as every poet knows. I was impressed with the poet hidden inside so many scientists, something I learned while doing research for two films and several magazine pieces. I found that the scientist in basic research needs the same outer life and inner life that a poet needs. Outwardly he wants a place to work in freedom and in tranquility, with time to moon, to let the imagination roam. Inwardly he needs inspiration, imagination, and the courage to dream great dreams. The scientist, as the poet, dare not be dull spirited. The layman tends to think of the scientist as devoid of emotion. Although no emotion shows in a lab report, that does not mean that emotions were absent when the findings were made. What is needed are more scientists, like Dr. Vishniac, who will share those emotions. That is a religious thing to do, a communication that is a form of worship.

I complained about too much fragmentation in education, but I think we have started to put things back together. Those crude divisions of nature, that we were so proud of, are being united into awkwardly named hybrids such as neuro-psychiatry, sociobiology, biophysics, and geopolitics. The economist now realizes he had better be interested in ecology and the ecologist knows he cannot ignore economics. And on and on as we put back together the fragments that hint of the magnificent mosaic. As Alan Watts said, "At a certain depth of specialization the divisions of scientific knowledge begin to run together because they are far enough advanced to see that the world itself runs together, however clear cut its parts may have seemed to be."

The more the scientist sees how the world runs together the more he is apt to develop the mystical spirit that comes with a deep awareness of beauty. It is natural for one of subtle pene-tration and strong spirituality to follow the path of Swedenborg, who moved from science into mysticism.

If Ruskin was right in believing that beauty is God revealed, then the scientist and the artist are involved in religion whether they will or no. Ruskin, believing that it is man's business to find God, gave lectures on political economy to encourage his countrymen to live more simply that they might live more beautifully. His concern was not with giving them more in-formation, but with more *formation,* and so his lectures were a form of religious instruction, although his audience never sus-pected.

Poetic vision is part of the imagination. Education ought to cherish imagination enough to try to develop it, if for no other reason than that the unimaginative life, like the unexamined life, is so cramped that getting through it is hardly worth the effort. It seems a man with an atrophied imagination couldn't be called educated, and yet some students graduate *summa cum laude* whose imaginations are vestigial. Such atrophy is inevitable when education does not put enough demands on the imagination.

Let's look at science and the imagination. I keep returning to science because the idea got around that matters of the spirit are for arts and letters and that too much concern for them might get in a scientist's way. I am not going to say how a science major should be taught, but I believe the student who is taking science as part of a humanities background needs information and vision, in equal doses. It is the vision that will influence his way of seeing things long after the formulae are forgotten for lack of use.

The vision of water given by Rachel Carson in *The Sea Around Us* and the information about water given by the chemist's formula, H_2O, sound like two different things, but each is an aspect of truth and each is worth knowing. The student who wants to be a professional scientist will have to face much hard-core information, and yet vision might not harm him, either. He might be a better scientist for it, a more complete person.

Planting information is easier than sharing a vision. The religion teacher wishes the student would go beyond the information of H_2O and realize that all water is holy. Yet, he too finds life simpler just going along planting information without trying to draw out too many realizations.

People who lack imagination on the secular side of life are apt to lack it in their encounter with God, too. Since imagination is an alertness to possibilities, an awareness of relationships that are less than evident, it takes imagination to see all things as a medium for an encounter with God. Unless things are seen this way we cannot take the admonition of Luke and Paul to pray at all times. To see this proper use of all things, this excellent temperance, is what Ignatius Loyola urged in his

Spiritual Exercises. If his idea has made little progress, the fault may lie more in lack of imagination than in ill will.

Since the imagination is a factor in seeing all of life as a possible encounter with God, religious education, even more than secular, needs be concerned with its development. Besides, it is through the imagination, that divine attribute, that man creates and in so doing imitates God the creator.

A theologian, the Rev. Robert Ochs, S.J., said that theology and spirituality, as they are now, suffer from not being sufficiently rooted in the imagination. Still, some writers concerned with the spiritual life say that reason alone can lead to a belief in God's existence, and that imagination leads to sentimentality for it tends to make pictures of the unpicturable. It is through the imaginative faculty, though, that one sees God reflected in here and now. Shakespeare, Homer, Dante, and Chaucer "saw the splendour of meaning that plays over the visible world," as Emerson observed. Such an angle of vision is a wordless alleluia straight from the heart. Prayer is not *knowing* God, but being *aware* of Him. It is not the mind that worships, but the person, the whole way of being.

While considering poetic vision, we can't ignore one of its by-products, a sense of mystery. Maybe a secular educator won't be too interested in mystery, but a religious educator just has to be. A sense of mystery is a part of faith, if faith means believing the unprovable. Since God is neither an observable It nor a finite I, but transcends every It and I, he has to be taken on faith. And yet one of the mysteries is that he reveals himself through finite things.

Theologians seemed a little embarrassed by mystery in a scientific age that thought only the provable worth considering. They started explaining God too much. They almost drew a sketch of Him and staked out the boundaries of heaven, hell, and purgatory, as though they were extensions of the new suburbia. Then came the latter-day theologian saying this is all wrong. But he, too, showed little interest in mystery; his interests were steeped in the social sciences and activism. Now he, also, is beginning to sound outdated. Like the hippie he is old-hat even in his prime.

The growing demand for a concern for feeling, for the intuitive, for the nonrational elements of faith are proving a new embarrassment for religious scholars who have come to feel at home in the world of reason. The dean of the Yale Divinity School, the Rev. Colin W. Williams, said at a symposium conducted at a seminary, "While the rational process of the universities has produced rich benefits and must be continued, we are sensing the inadequacies as well as the strengths of the university's intellectuality. A sense of mystery is sorely needed to restore life's balance and health."

An excess of rationality caused an imbalance that helped deaden the imagination. Atrophied imagination more than ill will or stubbornness may have put theologians, scientists, and artists at odds with one another. Lively imaginations would have revealed their common interests not evident at first glance. Instead, they argued about whether religion and science can abide each other and if perhaps religion and science are not natural enemies of art. Anyone taking part in such an argument today might be considered old-fashioned, unsophisticated, out of touch. Now all sides sense that they have more in common than they had suspected.

When articles about the conflict between religion and science were taking up space in popular magazines, any scientist who spoke of a professional concern for morality might be held suspect by his colleagues. Then came the atom bomb. The very physicists responsible for its development began to show concern about the right and wrong use of atomic energy, and when that concern entered their minds they were in the realm of morality. Now that biologists are capable of tampering with human genes, some of them wonder how much tampering is justified. Should psychologists alter human behavior? What about the moral problems that arise from psychosurgery?

There are also the matters of heart transplants, the use of DDT, abortion, euthanasia, all problems that can be filed under both science and morality. The scientist realizes that when he changes the environment and the human potential he is faced with moral concerns.

Maybe the scientist today is more apt than the theologian to develop a sense of mystery that verges on religious mysticism. The scientist's destiny is to invade the privacy of God's preserve, to reach large conclusions from small things, such as atomic energy, and to reduce large things to little formulae, $E=mc^2$. This sends him so deep into the realm of mystery that he is learning to say "maybe" more often than ever before. His arrogance of the past has been dispelled by the realization that what seems so sure today can be seen as naïve tomorrow. He agrees with Montaigne, who said that there is no practical matter on which anything more than an approximate solution can be had. This observation led Montaigne to skepticism, but it might well lead to reverence in its awareness of how remarkable creation is. As the British scientist Haldane said, "The universe is not only stranger than we suppose, it is stranger than we *can* suppose."

In his search for the knowable unknown, the scientist realizes that each time he opens a closed door he will face ten more closed doors and that behind each of those are ten more and so on *ad infinitum*. He can't help but gasp, if he has a spirit capable of going beyond scientific bookkeeping. In that gasp lies mysticism. There is no way of knowing how many scientists become mystics, because that grace is not displayed in the marketplace. There must be many mystics in the laboratory because of the hauntingness of God.

The groves of academe are more tranquil now that the scientist admits he has concerns beyond the provable. And the theologian is seeing the discoveries of science as revelation in our time. And the artist uses the discoveries of science as inspiration. The artist and theologian also better understand each other today than in 1959 when Father William Lynch, S.J., wrote *The Image Industries*. His recurrent theme was a plea for the creative theologian and the artist to get together because both have a desire in common—the true interpretation of man. Each wishes to say, in his own way, that man is a great and complicated and fascinating being. It is hard to understand why it took them so long to realize that they are both working the same side of the street in their mutual concern for a more sensitized spirit, and so are preparing an audience for each other. All they need is the imagination to tap each others' resources.

This must sound as though I want education to be blurred, vague, and amorphous—all of this talk about vibrating in the presence of quality, searching out a destiny, mystery and mysticism, imagination and intuition. It must seem as though I am promoting fun and games, and everybody doing his thing.

Anyone who has read this far must realize I am dismayed by formless teaching. The main business of education, as of any art, is to bring order out of chaos. Creation isn't chaotic, but our perception of it is. Alfred North Whitehead said that in the young child experience starts as a "blooming, buzzing confusion." And so he ought to be put in touch with some sort of order that develops the sense of design to introduce enlargement, significance, importance, and the delicacies of perception.

Teaching needs be based on what Whitehead calls "the accurate accomplishment of a succession of detailed tasks." To plan such tasks so that out of their definiteness will arise some vision takes an imaginative teacher. Otherwise, discipline can be a deadly order, or the pursuit of vision can be a fluttering of empty rhetoric. It takes an artist to impose a sense of order without making it a narrowing experience.

Teaching is an art. It is the most difficult, and the most important of all the arts, and yet it is never listed as one of the fine and liberal arts. If a man shapes clay into significant form or arranges pigment on a canvas in an effective way, he is called an artist. A teacher handles more important materials. He shapes attitudes, develops insights, stirs emotions, implants interest, shares information, enlarges judgments.

Just because someone knows subject matter is no guarantee that he can teach it. Years ago I learned this while bringing experts to my classroom. I was able to get, free of charge, effective journalists and broadcasters from New York. Their employers liked to list such guest lectures in the annual reports, and perhaps they used the expenses incurred as business deductions on income tax. Anyway, to get able people to appear in class was no trouble. However, the talks they gave would have been excellent for entertainment at a Rotary Club luncheon, but they had little to do with education.

Those experts could become good teachers, in time, if someone worked with them to show them how to use their imaginations to put what they know into a good order that communicates something to the student that will help him grow. This is what I think courses in education should be about, but hardly any of them are.

It all goes back to the fact that it is easier to teach content than sensitivity. The content goes a long way toward taking care of a teacher, no matter how poor his performance, but sensitivity puts the pressure directly on the teacher, and he stands or falls on his ability to communicate some angle of vision. The most perceptive criticism I ever heard a student make of a teacher came from a university senior who said, "He has no point of view." Perhaps the teacher did have a point of view, but his lack of design in each class session and in the courses as a whole kept all experience on the level of "a blooming, buzzing confusion."

An effective teacher develops an effective design for his course and ties in enough of other disciplines to hint at a larger mosaic. But first the teacher will have to put himself together inside. In this search for self-integration he can't depend too much on formal education, no matter if he is interested in secular or religious instruction. His will have to be a self-help project.

All the material he needs is at his disposal. It is found in the library, the museum, the gallery, the concert hall, the television screen, the motion picture screen. Take, for example, the public library: there are the plays, the novels, the findings of science, the recordings, the histories, the films, everything needed and just for the sake of the asking. There a teacher can range widely. In a short time he can explore areas that men gave their whole lives to exploring. After he has enough of these areas in mind he begins to see patterns form. It is work, for such insight is not given away with green stamps. Yet it is exciting work, this reading, looking, listening, fitting the jig-saw pieces together, putting fragments into a pattern.

Once he sees patterns form, his spirit expands. He feels more at ease with life. He senses that there is an order to things, that there is a plan in a disheveled world. Life is more than "fear in a handful of dust." This is an angle of vision that is a form of worship. Once the teacher has such an angle of vision he will pass it along without being aware of it. Perhaps such things that a student takes in by osmosis are the most valuable and enduring part of his education.

To be fair to educators, I must report that they have often shown concern for finding an angle of vision that will serve as a unifying force in the curriculum. They really want to raise schooling to the realm of education. Faculty committees have spent thousands of man-hours filling pages and pages with suggestions, reports that could only be printed after the destruction of thousands of trees. The reports are not remembered for as many years as it took the trees to grow.

I have never heard of a faculty committee that urged an awareness of design as a useful angle of vision to unify experience. Yet design is at once the most usual and unifying fact of creation. The scientist searches for it. The artist tries to impose significant form on bits and pieces. Mathematicians, historians, and social scientists have at rock bottom a concern for design. Politicians should be concerned with imposing an order on civil life. And each individual's life is a problem in design—that is what the next chapter is about.

9: Living Is an Art—
It Is Not Bookkeeping

Thirty-five years ago a line in a Saroyan play struck me, and I have recalled it often. A character in *The Time of Your Life* said, "Living is an art, it is not bookkeeping." This suggests that everybody's *magnum opus* can be the life he creates; whatever has been given him—talents, disposition, joys, sorrows—he needs to shape into some significance.

The well-formed life, like a work of art, communicates and worships through its way of being, a self-proclaiming morality. Just as a work of art has wholeness, a well-designed life has a wholeness that is called holiness. The characteristics of a well-designed life are those found in creation and in art: unity, variety, balance, harmony. Perhaps that is what the ancients meant when they often admonished, "live according to nature."

The need to create a well-designed life is a realization that goes deep into the past. The root of the Hebrew word *shalom* means being intact, complete, put together inside. To greet someone with "Shalom" means to wish him wholeness, hoping he is filled with the happiness that comes with being in harmony with self, nature, and God. It is asking that his life be a work of art.

Yom Kippur also has something to do with creating a holy life. The day of atonement is a time for a man to get back in

142

touch with God, to find his primary work, to see what he should be doing. This search for God's will is unifying; it brings an ever-unfolding sense of vocation.

A life, like schooling, can turn into an accumulation of fragments that never hints at the wholeness of a mosaic. Unless there is some sense of what we are meant to be, some abiding vision to give coherence to variegated experiences, and especially to all of those academic credits, life is just a cluttered attic.

To switch the metaphor, we might spend our days gathering ornaments but lack a Christmas tree to hang them on. The Christmas tree is our vision of God, man, and self. Our tree might be lopsided, blighted, and dismal, but it is better than nothing. It is better than having all those ornaments cluttering up the psyche and never adding up to anything.

Developing a unified angle of vision is a long process, unless you happen to be struck down on the road to Damascus, which today is more apt to come from a car than from a conversion. The angle of vision usually develops through creative searching. Like all creative work, such searching is long and hard and fraught with anguish, the price of creativity.

This matter of shaping a well-designed life, of finding a unity within one's self, is the personality evolution that analysts encourage in their patients. It is consoling to know that such formation can grow easier with the years. Living a well-designed life at seventy should be easier than at seventeen. By the time the declining years set in, if we have learned from our mistakes we may realize the rightness of such old-fashioned truths as the one about fame and fortune and fads not being satisfying.

No matter what our age, however, giving unity to the inner core must be harder now than in generations past, now that the old cultures have gone flying off in all directions like a fireworks display. Everyone over fifty remembers when Italians, Poles, Hungarians, Jews, Irish, Germans, and Greeks had their neighborhoods strongly united by pride, beliefs, traditions. Fraternal groups were full of energy. Farm life, too, had a traditional culture. Family trees were humble but sturdy. Everybody was born with a Christmas tree already set up for him, and all he needed do was to gather the ornaments and hang them on it. In those days the word *togetherness* was not heard. It has been much heard since World War II, and the more it is used the less there seems of it. Togetherness has moved to the suburbs, where it was turned bland as cultural roots lost their vitality.

Just as the rootless individual is more on his own to find himself, he is also more on his own to save himself. An old rabbi said, "As a young man I tried to save the world. In middle life I tried to save the community. Then I tried to save my family. Now that I am old I ask for the strength to save myself." He learned that trying to save himself was harder than trying to save the world. In confronting the world he could fool himself with a flurry of activity and a profusion of gobbledygook. He came to realize that after he had done something about himself he would be saving the world without knowing it. As Gandhi said, purification is highly infectious: "purification of oneself necessarily leads to the purification of one's surroundings."

The worst part of trying to save ourselves is facing up to ourselves. Realizing our inner dishevelment, seeing how lacking in good design our lives are, can be more disconcerting than facing a world full of imaginary enemies. It could take more courage, too.

While watching a television talk show I got to thinking about what a wonderful invention videotape is for anyone who wants to face his inner self. I wondered if those three women guests—a gossip columnist, a paramour, and a society psychoanalyst—were now at home watching the show and noticing what they had done to themselves through the years. They have grown unlovable: cunning, vicious, thick-skinned.

This would be noticeable even with the sound turned off. The camera doesn't need to show painful close-ups, either; all is evident even in medium shots. It would be less painful for those three to try to change the world—which they think they are doing—than to face their inner selves, to discover how lacking in inner design they are.

They too are caught in a culture that not only fails to offer a natural unity but fails to offer a natural variety as well. We can fool ourselves with great blurs of activity, believing it reflects a zestful variety. Life has become wheels within wheels like the prophet's vision. All of those people zooming across the freeways, with the landscape pouring past, are really hemmed in by dreary repetition. They are not active, not really. Theirs is a wild, disoriented passivity. And as for their inner lives, what seems to be variety may just be confusion. Their indecision, inconsistency, and whimsicality reflect a lack of stability, not a healthy variety.

The glory of many past cultures is that both secular and religious life moved to a common rhythm that provided an organic variety. Farming with its rhythms of the seasons and the liturgical year with its cycles of feasts formed a natural unity in the midst of variety.

Of course, even the unified cultures die in time, as is shown so graphically on the histomap I found hanging in the window of the second-hand bookshop in San Francisco. What probably happens is that traditionalism suffocates tradition. Since tradition exists in the midst of change, it must change and not just lie there inert, the way the traditionalists would have it. When tradition gives flavor and meaning and sense to the new it can thrive. When it stops doing that its end is in sight.

Now that a fragmented culture offers divertissements instead of creative variety, each person is stuck with creating his own rhythms and shaping his own unities. I find the academic life attractive because it is one of the few left that offers a rhythmic variety. The rhythms of the school year are definite and well spaced. In September begins the rising action: the world is young and everybody is making a fresh start filled with good intentions and high resolve; mistakes of the year before are in the past and here is a chance to begin anew. The tempo of the rising action depends on the design the teacher imposes on the course to keep it growing with unity in the midst of variety. A midsemester pause, and then the rising action continues until the final examination just before Christmas. The second semester repeats a similar rising movement climaxed by the high ritual of commencement. Then comes the sweet stillness of summer, a decided pause before the reuniting to create another cycle in the fall.

The need for variety to keep unity from being dull has been embedded in my consciousness ever since prep school days. Both textbook and teacher repeated "unity in the midst of variety" until it became a class joke. Yet I never realized so fully the importance of variety, how deadly a lack of it can be, until interviewing hundreds of retired people a few years ago.

In one respect retirees without enough money are better off than many with sufficient funds, because those without enough still foresee the possibility of variety in their lives. They can still wish and hope. They wish they had more money and they hope that if they get it all their problems will be solved. Many retired people with sufficient income no longer wish or hope. They can think of nothing that will free them from futility, aimlessness, purposelessness. All of their zestful human qualities have dried up and settled across their spirits as a gray bitterness. Today is as bland as yesterday. Tomorrow promises more sterility. They cannot wish or hope because those are creative acts that require imagination. Their imaginations have long dissolved. Even if they could imagine what to do, they are no longer willing to take the risk to make something happen. In such a state they are more apt to be against something than for it.

I used to know an elderly widow who suffered from a lack

of variety. She had money to spend and time to spend it and was under obligation to no one. She had the leisure and freedom people dream about. Yet she was so caged by fears, dissatisfactions, and uneasiness that to relieve the pressures she would, from time to time, declare war against life. A neighbor explained the widow's ways by saying, "Everybody needs drama in his life. If it doesn't come to him naturally he will create it. So she's creating it."

There is even a tendency to rebel against an environment that stays favorable too long. Paradise is easier to dream about than to live in. Perhaps it is too long on unity and too short on variety. Sooner or later comes a rage against affluence as an affront to our natures. To put it cruelly, human beings seem to need some difficulty. As Robert Frost used to say, "you have to have a chance to lose." Thackeray has a character say, "The best thing I can wish you, my child, is a little misfortune." A *little* misfortune, not a lack of it, because that in itself would be a misfortune. Without some misfortune the child would grow taller but would not grow up.

If difficulty does not come in the natural course of events it is created. Artificial difficulty is the hardest to bear; no one ever gets his fill of it. The artificial lacks something.

When people are faced with difficulties not of their making, they can rise to nobility. As a young newspaperman I learned that such misfortunes as floods, tornadoes, and fires bring out the best in people. When they are busy helping, excited by a new variety, they forget to gossip and bicker. As soon as the rubble is cleared away, they return to their old small selves.

Adventure, which means zestful variety, can be mental or physical, but the possibility has to be there. The intellectual may find it in reading philosophy or in scientific experiment; the more physical may need to open up new territory or ship off to sea. When the outlet appeals to someone he uses it to create something physical, or mental, or spiritual. If he finds nothing appealing he may use his need for variety to destroy.

The hunger for variety was suggested in a radio documentary about slum riots. In it young people used the word *bored* again and again, repeating, ''there's nothing happening.'' They said that basketball courts on playgrounds are all right, ''but you get tired of that.'' When they spoke of their roles in street riots they recalled them as great adventures, something that brought variety into a dull world.

Young people, especially, need a dramatic challenge to help them prove themselves and to help them feel there is a meaning in their lives. Without the right kind of outlet, being born in the suburbs can be almost as deadly as being born in the slums.

Suburbia can smother variety. That was the theme of a motion picture, *Bachelor in Paradise*. In it a writer, trying to get out of debt, begins a book *How Americans Live*. To gather material he moves into a planned community only to learn that this is a fate worse than debt.

The writer settles in Paradise Valley, California, where all of the houses went up at once and all look alike. Everybody in them tends to become as unimaginative as the setting. One sequence, done with military effect, shows how children are herded onto the school bus, and then, with speed-up photography, husbands rush into their driveways, swish their cars into the street to become droplets in a swollen river of traffic. Next, the housewives walk the dog, wheel the baby, borrow, and discuss.

The writer, appalled by the lack of grace and charm—words he fears will soon be listed as ''obsolete'' or ''archaic'' in the dictionary—tries to restore the amenities by starting a school for wives. He encourages them to avoid hair curlers and pre-prepared food, to try perfume, candles, and vintage wine for dinner, and to abandon slacks for dresses. When the husbands come home to these new conditions they are suspicious and uneasy.

In rebelling against their new-found variety, the husbands reveal the other side of the coin: some people rebel against

variety as much as some rebel for lack of it. Those seeking
security in the status quo try to stamp out surprises. In failing
to realize that security comes from within more than from
without, they are annoyed with any variety they meet along the
way, whether it be in theological thought, art, or cultures.

Yes, even theological thought was congealed for a time.
That everything about God has been settled once and for all
was the subject of a satiric short story, "Gideon Gunther and
God," published forty years ago in one of the little magazines.

Gideon Gunther, a theology student, is a simple, honest,
lovable fellow who has the virtues of a saint but lacks those of
a scholar. His theology grades are so sad that the rector of the
seminary calls Gideon to his office to give a last warning. The
rector says that Gideon will be given a special theology examination and that if he passes he will be welcome to stay, otherwise he must leave.

Gideon goes to the chapel to pray. As he prays an inner
voice says, "Fear not, Gideon, I will guide your hand." Sure
enough, during the theology examination Gideon's hand races
back and forth across the paper; words almost crackle as they
hit the page; he feels he is an instrument.

The next day the rector calls Gideon to his office. "I have
read your examination," he says. "In forty years of teaching I
have never seen so many strange answers. I fear you must
go."

The theology of Gideon's seminary rector was like a roast
beef dinner, definite and robust. Mysticism with its blurs and
vaguenesses was out of fashion, in those days, in a subject that
tried to be more dogma than mystery, more formula than wonder. Variety was kept in its place, mainly out of sight.

Now the oriental approach enjoys some favor. The feeling is
that maybe the best way to catch a glimpse of the Indescribable
is out of the corner of the eyes and that maybe God is best
approached by indirection rather than by frontal attack.

Why must it so often be a case of either/or—either intuition or intellect? By sensitizing the intuition, say through the arts, the spirit is open to insights and realizations that will not come with the fierce focus of intellect. But that doesn't mean the intellect should be spurned. It is an arrogance for anyone to think that he can scout God very thoroughly even with both intuition and intellect working overtime. In approaching the Almighty everybody needs variety more than he needs it for anything else in creation.

To define God too narrowly, to be too willing to utter the unutterable, shows a lack of the sense of the sublime. Yet it is only a sense of the sublime, an awareness of awe-inspiring variety, that keeps a theologian from creating God too much in his own image and likeness—a dull fellow.

Since Gideon Gunther's day both theologian and scientist have learned that the minute they become too dogmatic they are on the road to being second-rate. They realize there is more subtlety in the variety of creation than they had supposed. Perhaps this humility more than anything else has reconciled science with religion.

The scientist's approach to his subject is explained by Ritchie Calder in *Science in Our Lives:* "Every time he frames an hypothesis on the observable facts and says, 'Therefore, I believe such and such to be true;' it is a convenient supposition until his subsequent experiments prove or disprove it, and then belief becomes a *fact*—but never a *certainty,* because subsequent knowledge may modify his conclusion. (Newton's Laws looked like a statement of certainty, but they have been modified by Einstein.)"

The scientist realizes, and the philosopher and theologian must face it too, that no matter how much he learns about a given thing he always leaves something for the next generation to discover. He knows that if a thousand scientists study the atom for a thousand years they will become even more aware of what they don't know about it. The great variety of creation will always keep everybody well short of definitive knowledge.

People who cherish variety, who know that change is inevitable, and who keep growing in spirit form an unofficial brotherhood. They recognize each other as readily as do fraternity brothers who share secret signs and meaningful handshakes. Teilhard de Chardin hinted at this when he wrote in a letter, "Whatever the country, the creed or the social position of the person I approach, so long as the same fire of expectancy glows in him as it does in me, then a fundamental, final and total contact is immediately established."

To glow with the "fire of expectancy" is to know the awe of sharing in an ever-unfolding creation. It is more than a resignation to variety; it is a love of it as one of the characteristics that God stamped into creation.

This means facing without flinching some of the uncomfortable prospects of change. For instance, facing the fact that a culture and a civilization are as passing as people, and that the human race, composed of mortal man, is not everlasting either. It means admitting that if a bomb destroys all of life it is a part of the logic of morality. Maybe that happened on other stars a million times and will happen a million times again. This may be a part of variety.

Since our fragmented culture offers scant unity and a thin, unsatisfactory variety, it can't be expected to offer much by way of balance, either. The Greek philosophers felt that balance is the hardest thing in life to come by and anyone who has lived and breathed a few years on earth might be inclined to agree. To teeter on the sharp edge of reality, like a tightrope performer in the circus, is only human but to go flying off to one extreme or another is dehumanizing. In an extreme position one first becomes a caricature, a parody of self, and then a fanatic.

The dehumanizing effect of fanaticism is the central theme of Eric Hoffer's book *The True Believer*. He explores the psychology of extremists, especially those in religion and political life.

The deadliness of fanaticism is revealed in a brilliantly conceived scene in Ingmar Bergman's *The Seventh Seal*. A procession of religious fanatics are whipping each other and carrying on something fierce. Bergman holds the camera quiet until the procession clears the frame, and then quite deliberately he tilts down and holds for some time on a patch of parched earth. Through this juxtaposition of the fanatics and parched earth he helps us realize that the out-of-balanced can make the same boast made by the Mongol hordes, "Where we ride the grass will never grow again!"

Whether there are really more out-of-balance people now than in the past, or whether it just seems that way, I don't know. Maybe they seem more numerous because the technical advances in communication and transportation have made them more visible and more heard. They telephone radio talk shows, write letters to the editor, get themselves on TV discussion programs, and, in general, use the media to grind their little axes. With jets and automobiles they can hurriedly assemble anywhere in the country and give the impression that their numbers are greater than they are. It gets tiresome seeing all of those intense, inflammatory, and highly vibratory people, day after day, acting as though the whole course of civilization depends on whether or not they get their way. They have a knack for stamping out serenity, their greatest enemy.

Since the extremists have the touch that kills, they are the worst enemies of their own cherished causes. They make what they promote so repulsive that anyone with a sense of balance wants to flee, even though the cause may have merit. It then becomes a case of the unbalanced being attracted to the unbalanced.

What makes a fanatic so unlovable is his arrogance. Pride has outbalanced humility. A Hasidic master wrote that everyone must have two pockets, "In his right pocket he must keep the words 'For my sake was the world created,' and in his left, 'I am dust and ashes.'"

Perhaps all of life should be lived with the balanced double awareness of the Gregorian chants for the Christmas season. They see Christmas as a warm festival, but also in their dignity, solemnity, and splendor they prepare the way for Lent. From the First Sunday of Advent to the Sixth Sunday after the Epiphany bursts of joy are balanced by a spirit aware of the inevitability of the cross.

Extremists are usually unbalanced on the side of pessimism. Our grandfathers, filled with the bland confidence of the Emersonians, were unbalanced on the side of optimism. Why we shifted from one extreme to the other I don't know. Perhaps the mass media, in covering the world like the morning smog, had something to do with it. Our grandfathers knew negative news, but technology had not yet developed to the point where it could completely saturate them with it.

A newspaper somewhere in Pennsylvania used to publish only good news on the front page on Christmas Eve. The front page that one day of the year was an inaccurate reflection of the way life is, but no more inaccurate than the rest of the days when darkness is the prevailing theme. If we baled up all the newspapers and magazines for one week and taped all the radio and television newscasts for that week and sent the whole package to Mars, wouldn't it give the Martians an unbalanced idea of life on earth? To put it another way, if we wanted to let the Martians know what a human being looks like, we would send the picture of a man and a woman showing them from head to foot and not settle for close-ups of sores and distortions, which are a part of reality but not all of it.

This sounds like hogwash to extremists who specialize in the negative in their frontal attacks on anything that gets in the way. They lack the sensitivity, or the sense, to realize that frontal attacks are not always best. Certainly they must have noticed that they can't get happiness by making a frontal attack on it. Happiness is a by-product that comes from a life stamped with decency. Love, too, won't be won by grim determination. It comes only to those who have made themselves able to give love and able to receive it.

What is appalling in the grimly alienated is their lack of tolerance. They don't seem to realize that change wrought through intolerance will be just as out of balance as the thing changed and that one good cannot be bought at the expense of others. The imbalance that comes from lack of tolerance is reflected in the attitude of a student at Antioch college who called himself a revolutionary in residence. In a network television program he said with fervor that all universities ought to be the way one in Bologna was a few hundred years ago: "Teachers had to get permission from the students to leave the campus. Sometimes the teachers were locked in stocks. That's the way it has to be here!"

Such lack of balance makes the radical right and the radical left brothers under the skin. They are alike in narrowness and shallowness. With clichés and arrogance each extremist generates energy for one purpose, to force others to conform, for they are the greatest conformists around. Walter Lippmann pointed out that the radical right goes one way 180 degrees and the radical left the other way 180 degrees and when they meet near the bottom they are both so unbalanced that they are not easily distinguishable.

Harmony in a fragmented society is as hard to come by as unity, variety, and balance. Since harmony is the fitness and rightness of things, it has to do with physical well-being, mental health, serenity, appreciation, and a thousand other things in daily life. Its presence, or lack of it, shows up in so many ways that it is difficult to know where to start talking about it.

Perhaps three homey but off-beat anecdotes will serve as a beginning in observing the vast possibilities of harmony:

A colleague of mine was eating in a crowded railroad diner when the steward seated a middle-aged woman across the table from him. She took one look at my friend's plate and said, "What a horrible color combination!" She explained that she is a specialist in nutrition and that anyone ignorant in matters nutritional would do well to select food by color. A plate harmoniously balanced in color—one aesthetically pleasing in its greens, reds, yellows, whites, and browns—is apt to be well-balanced nutritionally.

The same colleague knew a landscape architect who volunteered for naval duty in World War II, saying he wanted to go to sea because there he could study clouds. Landscape architects, he explained, steal some of their best ideas from cloud formations, because while studying those harmonious masses the architects sensitize themselves to create more harmonious silhouettes out of trees, bushes, and shrubs.

Another example of how harmony comes into daily life was described by Oliver Messiaen when he said, "Birds are the greatest musicians. You will never find in their song a mistake in rhythm, melody or counterpoint." So Messiaen, an *avant garde* composer of twentieth-century music, tramps through the woods of France making notes of bird songs to find themes for new compositions.

The nutritionist, the landscape architect, and the composer all search nature for a harmony they can use. Each has learned, within the limits of his specialty, that when somebody steals from God he is the better for it. It is possible that a specialist will learn this in the area of his expertise but fail to apply it to all of life.

Sometimes the inharmonious clash between God's work and man's is found in places where the clash seems sacrilegious. For example, I visited a seminary in Hawaii that is blessed with a lagoon kept brimming by a wonderful waterfall. The seminarians turned the lagoon into a swimming pool with a hard-edged concreteness that nearly obliterates the hand of God. Had they sought the help of a Japanese gardener he would have transformed the lagoon into a suitable swimming pool with enough harmonious transitions at the edges to keep God in the plan. Eliminating God from the plan might be a moral problem that could be discussed in the seminary classroom.

This brings to mind another group of seminarians who also showed the need for a better developed sense of harmony. During a screening of the film *The Gospel According to Saint Matthew,* they laughed at the apostles for not being the glamorized actors with capped teeth, nose jobs, hairpieces and makeup seen in the Hollywood biblical spectaculars. They were unprepared for rough-hewn men with bent noses and chipped teeth, looking the way common men have always looked. The seminarians have had their sense of harmony vulgarized by a vulgar culture. They fail to recognize a certain kind of truth when they meet it, and yet each one who laughed is probably prepared to define truth in a philosophy exam.

This lack of sense of harmony in seminarians seems especially painful. They are supposed to be getting ready to proclaim God as the Creator of the Universe and the Author of Life and so lead people along the way to a proper harmony. For a religious to be insensitive and insubmissive to nature is ironic. To develop such sensitivity, seminarians probably need to give as much attention to art as philosophy. This may help them read the messages embedded in creation, especially the message of harmony as a form of revelation.

Everybody needs all of the help he can get to develop this sense of harmony. Our lack of such shows in our abuse of technology. Instead of using technology as a servant we have become its slave.

The Athenians used servants to give them the leisure and comfort needed to lift the cultural level. Someone estimated that technology gives us the cumulative effort of about four hundred servants. With all of that help we should be able to develop the most humanistic culture the world has ever known. Since a well-developed sense of harmony is supposed to be the mark of a humanist, perhaps only he can use technology with sense and reason.

The humanistic flame burns low in our time. Instead of using comfort and leisure for inner growth, we use it to clutter up the earth with fun and games: cars cluttering up the streets, the all-too-many sports shows on television, the excessive number of entertainment programs, the great ticket sales for all kinds of hoopla. Pollution, shortages of every kind, crime, and accidental deaths result from an abuse of providential gifts. All gifts turn terrible in bad hands. Then comes the price to pay, *hubris*.

The inharmonious use of inanimate objects is reflected in the cluttered approaches to our cities. This insensitivity to material, this lack of respect for the medium, shows in a lack of civilized craftsmanship, a defective sense of harmony. Such cluttered approaches lack the harmony of art because they are monuments to selfishness. Good craftsmanship demands a certain kind of humility, a respect and a love for the material used, a willingness to let the self serve as an interpreter of the medium, a searching self rather than a domineering self.

When the archeologists dig us out of the ruins—and sooner or later every civilization contributes its share to the ruins—we may not be judged as civilized as we think we are. The diggers will find our spirits reflected in a bewilderment of highways and slick shopping centers more than in our churches. They are not apt to label our times as the Golden Age of Design.

A revolt against the characteristics of good design—unity, variety, balance, harmony—may be a reflection of man's fallen nature. This revolt in art, and in the life of an individual, is a recurring motif in history. The revolt against unity, for example, comes as a reaction when unity is pushed so far it reaches immobility. Such rebelling shows up in the theater, films, writings, painting, all of man's creative efforts. It shows also in the way individuals shape their lives.

Form-breaking theater of a decade ago was a revolt against what used to be called "the well-made play." In writing, at the time, about the decline of form in the theater, Walter Kerr, drama critic of the New York *Times,* described *Tom Paine,* one of the plays that asks the actors to improvise quite a bit:

> Paul Foster's *Tom Paine* insists that the actors be forced out every now and again, actually thrust from the play to make their own lines as they chat with the people who have paid to see them.
>
> Let's say that we have been watching and listening to four actors hop about the stage while one beats a drum, three ride another piggy-back, two Tom Paines mutter in unison in the background, and all talk at once. That's the play proper. Its effect is ritualistic-cum-impressionist but it is written. Now one of the company says, "Do let us pause and cool the stage," and all performers go slack, letting the effort of being important go out of them, as they drape feet over the apron's edge and begin to say whatever comes into their heads.
>
> The whole purpose of form-breaking, of course, is to reawaken that spiritually dead audience out there, to shock it into a recognition that it is *related* to something really going on, to bring it alive. I must say that the technique worked. Some members of the audience came so alive that they left. Others expressed themselves more emphatically and even more coherently than the actors.

The revolt against design was found in films, too, especially in underground movies. Theatrical films showed some form-breaking tendencies, but they were so expensive that there was less willingness among those financing them to experiment with artistic anarchy. It is true that the glory of many theatrical films was the glory of the technician and nothing more: the picture was excellent; sound quality, excellent, color balance, excellent, but there was precious little for the spirit because the films were manufactured more than created. Let a certain type of film do well at the box office and others like it were ground out with little to recommend them except technical know-how.

Experimentalists, I suppose, became nauseated at the sight of so many skilled technicians working hard to present the shallow. So they revolted against technique, seeking comfort in the cult of the self-consciously obscure, the "spontaneous," the formless.

Some formless work, such as *Last Year at Marienbad,* may exude an aura of quality that has value in itself. That French film, instead of presenting a story in recognizable dramatic form, offered ninety-three minutes of vaguely related images. In it a man wandered through long corridors in a massive, baroque hotel heavy with nineteenth-century, central European grandeur. He passed through crowded rooms, gathering snippings of conversations, and he held long stream-of-consciousness conversations with a woman he claimed he had met last year at Marienbad. At first she denied they had met, but then began to wonder if perhaps she was wrong. All of this is told in a hop-skip-and-jump sort of way, in the way the mind works in remembering.

A printed program given at the door read, "While viewing this film of rare visual beauty, you will want to give a meaning to what you see, but your neighbor may perhaps find an entirely different one."

It was enjoyable to take such exquisite bits and pieces and assemble them in some order. Perhaps it was also enjoyable to take the fragments offered by the form-breaking novelist whose "book" was published as a clutter of loose pages in a box with the hope that the reader would select the pages at random making of them whatever he was able.

The form-breakers, in asking the audience to do the work, put hope in the happy accident, which is a part of the gamble in all art. But they push it too far. Someone asked Edward Steichen how many of his great photographs were happy accidents and he said "Quite a few, but a good photographer has more happy accidents than a poor photographer." The glory of the happy accident follows the discipline of the craftsman. This is a truth of technique that anyone learns who attempts water colors, the art form that depends more on the happy accident than any other. Audience participation pushed too far demands more of chance than anyone has a right to ask.

Do-it-yourself art, promoted by the form-breakers, can be interesting and fun on occasion and good calisthenics for the imagination. But it can be a gimmick, too, and an unfairness, as though an architect delivered mounds of bricks and stone to a vacant lot and told his client to go ahead and assemble them into a building. It might give the client much needed exercise, but the architect would be letting himself off too easily.

The best artists if they break an old form create a new one, because they know intuitively that finding an effective form is the price paid for superb communication. An English writer said that every piece of writing is hard on somebody, either writer or reader, and it is the writer's job to make things as unencumbered for the reader as possible. She said that she writes everything four times: the first time, to get it down on paper; the second to put in what was omitted on the first writing; the third to take out everything that should not have been there to start with, and the fourth to make it all sound as though she had just thought of it.

Tolstoi said "One must always reject the idea of writing without correction. Three or four drafts are not enough." I often think of his wife with compassion. She used to copy his drafts in longhand. Imagine after she had recopied *War and Peace* several times how she must have cringed to see the old boy pick up the manuscript and start scribbling on it. No wonder the Tolstois did not get along very well.

In avoiding responsibility for design, the creative man is avoiding the kind of charity he is meant to bring into the world. Anthony Burgess said that "one of the jobs of art is to persuade us that life has a pattern." T. S. Eliot felt that the ultimate function of art is "to bring us to a condition of serenity, stillness, and reconciliation." This is done, he said, by helping us, through a well-wrought piece of work, to perceive order in reality. This perception helps us "climb the cross of the moment," to use a line from Auden. Such help is a moral function, bringing us consolation. It is the kind of charity praised in the beatitudes.

The form-breakers, spiritual heirs of the old iconoclasts, may be protesting against slick banalities. A protest against the uninspired and the insincere is praiseworthy, but so often the protesters develop a brand of phoniness all of their own.

All of those "instant artists" approve of things that lack technique, lack design, because such things are within their range of competence. They prefer films, poems, paintings, and plays that the unaccomplished can produce. It is convenient for instant artists to favor amateurism over professionalism, because professionalism requires imagination, personal discipline, and hard work, something they are not willing to put themselves through. It is easier to take the attitude that anything they do is wonderful simply because they do it.

False standards on the sending end, the artist's end, are bad enough but false standards on the receiving end are even worse. The audience, the receiving end, so often likes something for the wrong reason that honest professionalism can be a disadvantage. For example, *Life* magazine ran an interview with an author who worked hard to make a book as dirty as possible. He rigged it every step of the way with his audience constantly in mind. The author considered the book a great "in" joke on a stupid world. This rigging of something is not a rarity in mass communication.

Lack of standards turns life into a confusion of fads. A young woman reviewing a record said, "It is already dated because its release was delayed a year. It sounds '72 and '73." This was in June of '74. The "NOW" films of the late 60s are more dated than the films of D. W. Griffith, a director who had some standards early in this century.

None of this is new though, at least not in light of what Plato wrote: "The only standard today is the pleasure of the hearers, no matter what sort of men they are. Those are blind who have no clear standard, and the divine is the eternal measure."

When the cult of the formless rode high, Walter Kerr wrote, "Shape will come again, if only because man's mind has an instinct for putting building blocks on top of one another until they make a pyramid. I find, as I talk to university students here and there across the country, that the itch for shapes, for form, for control of the new materials, stirs irresistibly."

Hardly had he written those sentences when shape was back again. Nostalgia came in with a vengeance, a case of the pendulum swinging to the other extreme. This, too, is getting out of balance. First it was *No, No Nannette,* nostalgia for the '20s; then came *The Summer of '42;* next, *Grease,* nostalgia for the '50s. Today an ad for *American Graffiti* asks, "Where were you in '62?" Soon we will run out of years and will have to be nostalgic for last November.

Without visiting universities Mr. Kerr would have been confident of design's return because he knows something of history. For one thing he knows that a return to the old always makes people who know nothing of the past think they are in the presence of something new. He knows that every angle of vision has some built-in obsolescence: the radical theologian, the Thomists, the existentialists—none of their visions survive to be accepted in their entirety, because only God has any given area cased completely. The Impressionists revolted against the academicians. Cezanne revolted against the Impressionists and gave birth to the Cubists. When nonrepresentational painters revolted against representational painting the *avant garde* said that no one would take representational painting seriously again. Then came a new *avant garde,* the pop artists, who took themselves seriously while painting representational soup cans and bottles. The cycle always wins.

Those who sense a need for variety find it difficult to move with fairness from what was acceptable in the past to a new way of doing things in the present. In an essay in *Christian Reflections* C. S. Lewis wrote this perceptive paragraph:

There are some mistakes which humanity has made and repeated so often that there is now really no excuse for making them again. One of these is the injustice which every age does to its predecessor; for example, the ignorant contempt which the Humanists (even good Humanists like Sir Thomas More) felt for medieval philosophy, or Romantics (even good Romantics like Keats) felt for eighteenth-century poetry. Each time all of this 'reaction' and resentment has to be punished and unsaid; it is a wasteful performance. It is tempting to try whether we, at least, cannot avoid it. Why should we not give our predecessors a fair and filial dismissal?

The rebellion against the order of our predecessors was especially vehement between 1965 and 1970, overflowing from the gallery, the movie house, the theater, onto the street and campus. Chaos was enshrined. All of that fierceness has run its course for the moment. As this is being written there seems to be better unity, variety, balance, and harmony in life than a decade ago. Yet by the time this is published we may have gone whooping off to some other extreme. Our amino acid is charged with such terrible intensity. Whether the next extreme will be to the right or the left is not clear today, Monday, but by Thursday it may all have happened. Another case of lemmings rushing into the sea. One thing is sure, in the pursuit of wisdom the paths are never crowded.

If that sounds cynical, remember that cynicism comes easily to anyone who reads history or pays attention to the mass media. Sometimes I feel cynical in agreeing with Roch Nicholas Chamfort, who said that although he had been taught that the beginning of wisdom is the fear of God, he had come to believe that the beginning of wisdom is the fear of man. (As it turned out, during the man-inspired Reign of Terror he was beheaded by a man-made, man-operated guillotine.) Yet I feel optimistic in agreeing with Vladimir Nabokov that each human life is a footnote in a vast, obscure unfinished masterpiece. Anyone who sees the great script as a masterpiece cannot consider it absurd.

To avoid cynicism one needs to believe in the perfectibility of man, or to see all events as part of a divine script, the mysterious unfolding of a purpose that will ultimately be fulfilled. I lean toward the divine script.

This sounds like a denial of free will but not if free will is tactical rather than strategic. Men and nations can do and not do, push and pull, shape and reshape, in their own limited ways, that's tactical. But the over-all strategic plan is beyond them. So an individual is free to lead a chaotic life, a shabby work of art, yet still be caught up in a beautifully designed pattern that is beyond his spoiling.

Such an amazing plan is what the histomap hinted at hanging there in the window of the secondhand bookstore in San Francisco. In showing the rise and fall of civilizations over the past four thousand years, it revealed a unified design. And that is why it has haunted me ever since.

Reading That's Worth the Effort

Mortimer Adler, *Great Ideas from the Great Books* (New York: Washington Square Press, Inc., 1961).

Bernard Basset, S.J., *Let's Start Praying Again* (Garden City, N.Y.: Doubleday Image Book, 1973).

Bernard Basset, S.J., *The Noonday Devil* (Fresno, Calif.: Academy Guild Press, 1964).

Bernard Berenson, *Aesthetics and History* (Garden City, N.Y.: Doubleday & Company, Inc., Anchor Book, 1954).

Bernard Berenson, *Sunset and Twilight* (New York: Harcourt Brace and World, 1963).

David Bergamini, *Mathematics* (New York: Life Science Library, Time, Inc., 1963).

Christopher Booker, *The Neophiliacs* (London: Fontana, 1970).

Jerome S. Bruner, *The Process of Education* (New York: Vintage Books, a division of Random House, 1960).

Ritchie Calder, *Science in Our Lives* (New York: Signet Science Library Books published by The New American Library of World Literature, Inc. revised printing, 1962).

Betsy Caprio, *Experiments in Prayer* (Notre Dame, Ind.: Ave Maria Press, 1973).

Epictetus, *Discourses,* trans. Thomas Wentworth Higginson (Roslyn, N.Y.: Walter J. Black, Inc., 1944).

Martin Gardner, ed., *Great Essays in Science* (New York: Washington Square Press, 1957).

Maitland Graves, *The Art of Color and Design* (New York: McGraw-Hill, 1951).

Dom Bede Griffiths, *The Golden String* (Garden City, N.Y.: Doubleday Image Book, 1964).

Dag Hammarskjöld, *Markings,* trans. by Leif Sjoberg and W. H. Auden (New York: Knopf, 1964).

Eric Hoffer, *The True Believer* (New York: Harper, 1951).

William James, *The Varieties of Religious Experience* (New York: Collier Books, 1961).

Ralph E. Lapp, *Matter* (New York: Life Science Library, Time, Inc., 1965).

C. S. Lewis, *The Screwtape Letters* (New York: Macmillan, 1943).

William Lynch, S.J., *The Image Industries* (New York: Sheed & Ward, 1959).

Marcus Aurelius, *Meditations* with introduction by Irwin Edman (Roslyn, N.Y.: Walter J. Black, Inc., 1945).

Edgar Lee Masters, *The Living Thoughts of Ralph Waldo Emerson* (New York: Fawcett World Library, 1958).

Henry Margenau and David Bergamini, *The Scientist* (New York: Life Science Library, Time, Inc., 1964).

Rollo May, *Love and Will* (New York: W. W. Norton & Co., 1969; London: Fontana, 1972).

Thomas Merton, *The Sign of Jonas* (New York: Harcourt Brace, 1953).

Michel de Montaigne, *Selected Essays,* trans. Donald M. Frame (Roslyn, N.Y.: Walter J. Black, Inc., 1943).

Edwin Newman, *Strictly Speaking* (Indianapolis, Ind.: Bobbs-Merrill, 1974).

Robert Ochs, S.J., *God Is More Present Than You Think* (New York: Paulist Press, 1970).

José Ortega y Gasset, *The Revolt of the Masses* (New York: W. W. Norton, 1957).

Plato, *Dialogues,* trans. W.H.D. Rouse, ed. Eric H. Warmington and Philip G. Rouse (New York: New American Library Mentor Book, 1956).

Plutarch, *Selected Lives and Essays,* trans. Louise Ropes Loomis (Roslyn, N.Y.: Walter J. Black, Inc., 1951).

James D. Shaughnessy, ed., *The Roots of Ritual* (Grand Rapids, Mich.: Eerdmans, 1973).

Robert L. Short, *The Gospel According to Peanuts* (Richmond, Va.: John Knox Press, 1965).

William Strunk and E. B. White, *The Elements of Style* (New York: Macmillan, 1959).

Adrian van Kaam, *Religion and Personality* (Englewood Cliffs, N.J.: Prentice-Hall, 1964).

Ritchie Ward, *The Living Clocks* (New York: Knopf, 1971; New American Library, 1972).

Evelyn Waugh, *Ronald Knox* (London: Chapman & Hall, 1959).

Films for the Spirit

The films mentioned in this book are listed, along with the rental fee when quoted in the catalog, and the abbreviated name of the distributors whose names and addresses follow the listing.

Anytime, 29 min, b & w, $16.90, NUFL
The Circle, 57 min, b & w, $25.00, CONT
Cosmic Zoom, 8 min, color, $12.50, CONT
Cross Country Runner, 14 min, b & w, $11.00, UCEMC
A Dancer's World, 33 min, b & w, UCEMC
Dancing Prophet, 22 min, color, $15.00, ASF
Death of a Salesman, 111 min, b & w, CPC
The Eucharistic Prayer of Hippolytus, 60 min, color, $25.00, ASF
Goodnight, Socrates, 39 min, b & w, $15.00, VIEW
The Gospel According to Saint Matthew, 136 min, b & w, $125.00, ABF
The Great Holiday Massacre, 54 min, b & w, $23.50, AIM
The Hat, 18 min, color, $19.00, UCEMC
The Heart Is a Lonely Hunter, color, WB
The House, 32 min, b & w, $30.00, CONT
Ikiru (To Live), 140 min, b & w, $75.00, ABF
La Dolce Vita, 180 min, b & w, $122.50, MAB
La Strada, 107 min, b & w, $80.00, JAN
A Light for John, 29 min, b & w, $6.50, USC
Man of Aran, 77 min, b & w, $35.00 CONT
Nanook, 55 min, b & w, $24.00, UCEMC
On the Waterfront, 108 min, b & w, $50.00, MAIP
Overture/Nyitany, 10 min, color, $5.50, KSU

The Quiet One, 66 min, b & w, $17.50, KSU
The Red Kite, 17 min, color, $22.50, VIEW
Requiem for a Heavyweight, 85 min, b & w, $25.00, CONT
The River, 13 min, b & w, $4.00, IU
The Set Up, 77 min, b & w, FI
The Seventh Seal, 96 min, b & w, $125.00, JAN
The Stray, 14 min, color, $15.00, ASF
String Bean, 17 min, color, $17.50, CONT
Umberto D, 89 min, b & w, $125.00, JAN
War on Gobbledygook, 27½ min, color, OFMP
Wilf, 15 min, color, $15.00, CONT
William, 13 min, color, $15.00, ASF

Association Instructional Materials
512 Burlington Avenue, LaGrange, IL 60525

Association Sterling Films
512 Burlington Avenue, LaGrange, IL 60525

Audio Brandon Films
8400 Brookfield Avenue, Brookfield, IL 60513

Columbia Picture Corporation
16mm Sales Division
711 Fifth Avenue, New York, NY 10017

Contemporary Films
Princeton Road, Highstown, NJ 08520

Films Inc.
733 Greenbay Road, Wilmette, IL 60091

Indiana University
Audio Visual Center, Bloomington, IN 47401

Janus Films, Rental Distribution
745 Fifth Avenue, New York, NY 10022

Kent State University
Audio Visual Services, Kent, OH 44242

Macmillan Audio Brandon
8400 Brookfield Avenue, Brookfield, IL 60513

Macmillan/Audio Ideal Pictures
1712 N. Illinois Street, Indianapolis, IN 46202

Northwestern University Film Library
P.O. Box 1665, Evanston, IL 60204

OFM Productions
1229 South Santee, Los Angeles, CA 90015

University of California Extension Media Center
2223 Fulton Street, Berkeley, CA 94720

University of Southern California
Film Distribution Center, Los Angeles, CA 90007

Viewfinder Films
P.O. Box 1665, Evanston, IL 60204

Warner Brothers Non-Theatrical Division
4000 Warner Blvd., Burbank, CA 91503